Say, What?

"The Lost Art of Communication"

...communicate!

Say, What?

"The Lost Art of Communication"

Leon McWhorter

iv Say, What?

-----Contents-----

2 Say, What?

For Campbell John and Reid William
communicators of the future

Preface

Meaningful communication appears to be on life support. I'm not sure if the dilemma is because so many are uneducated, unaware, or simply don't care. Regardless, the ability to communicate effectively in business, socially, and personally is rapidly becoming another fond memory from *the good old days*. If you even marginally agree, read on.

Perhaps communicating verbally is integral to your professional or personal roles. Maybe you need to improve your live delivery of presentations. Or, perhaps your messaging lacks impact or audience retention. If so, this book is for you. Because, you understand, it all begins with a story and the drama of daily life. We are the sum of our collective parts. The challenge is how to determine if our messaging is adding up.

In our email, text, chat, IM, social media, and limitations of 140 characters to elaborate on our mission, the art of speaking is falling away. At even greater peril is the apparent loss of our ability to communicate effectively in business and in our private lives. If you find that troubling, read on; if not…"Thanks for stopping by, TTYL, may you and your BFF rest in your BAM while I go B2W."

There was a time, not long ago, when high value was placed on face-to-face conversation—not FaceTime the app, but face time with faces instead. This was a time when people were interested in hearing before speaking and listening before reacting. Acknowledging varied points of view held not only validity, but value. In my travels and addressing varied groups of professional communicators, I find these desires are still present. But, we seem to have lost the implementation process. We know we need to know, but can't understand why we can't understand. Say, what? It's an enigma really. Does it really have to be that way? I think there's hope of restoration of talents found in the communication fundamentals we all know but have somehow allowed modern technology to erode. Here's believing we can find our way back to where we started, to enhance where we are going.

A story is told of Vince Lombardi, former coach of the Green Bay Packers, the same guy the Lombardi trophy is named after and awarded to the winners of the big football game. I can't say the name of the game as copyright laws prevent me from doing so, but, I think you get it. After a particularly bad season, the legend goes that, at training camp the following year, this great man held up a football and announced to his team, "Gentlemen, time to get back to basics. This is a football" in an effort to illustrate the value of fundamentals. Regardless of the validity of the tale, it is a great lesson to us all to recall the basics of communication before we allow the acronyms and brevity of technology to claim us.

Ladies and gentlemen, this is where drama meets communication. This is where the power of words is understood, the intent realized, relationships forged and successes far past those of monetary value are achieved.

This is relationship development—the cornerstone of success and continued personal and professional fulfillment. This is the stuff we know but forget to implement. This is life meeting demand. Say, what? Read on.

Chapter 1 – Media

Before we can work on where we want to go, we must first agree on how we arrived where we are. Unlike any generation prior, this has been one built on the backs of technology. Much of this was driven by our self-proclaimed need to be entertained while educated. "Edu-tainment" (I'm not sure who coined that word) is indeed a model more and more prevalent in communications. However, this desire to relate dramatically is not new. Note: There is a difference between relating and being entertained. Entertainment often involves acting whereas relational realities are based in the drama we call living. We are all dramatic but not all actors. Say, what?

8 Say, What?

As a communicator, you allow the reality of your experiences to enhance your ability to present. While we have greater access to information today, some say this access has actually diminished our abilities to relate to one another. Consequently, we find ourselves at the doorsteps of a personal society with limited social skills and awareness. In other words, we are the sum of our collective media relationships as opposed to our live interactions with others of the species.

Our personalities have been forged on all platforms. We need to acknowledge their power as well as understand the value of lessons learned while embracing the potential they offer. These are the formative agendas that shape our ability to communicate on wide levels—if we only acknowledge the skills they offer.

Since the dawn of time, drama has been an integral part of communication. The caveman drew on the walls of his domicile to aid in relating to his fellow cave dwellers. Native Americans sat fireside and recalled the day's travels and times gone by. Today, we still gather in the glow of many glittering blue lights to experience the drama that is life—the drama that is communication, the drama that can drain us of our skills needed to thrive—if we allow it.

The challenge is to control the input and manipulate the information for our good instead of allowing the data to deconstruct our abilities for elaborative thinking. Facts are facts, true, but, the molding and delivery of those facts resonate. It's not too late! Before we delve into fleshing out our ideas and dreams, we need to first take a peek behind the scenes of what drives us so we might better drive results for those we serve. Please note that the term, "serve," was not used by accident.

> *Great communicators are WE-centric, never ME-centric.*

Stage

In the world of communication, there really is no more dramatic, **intimate** arena than the private room known by actors as "the space" but, to the rest of us, the theater is often a place of refuge. In this darkened hall, we sit surrounded by others, yet alone, bringing our personal expectations and group motivations. We speak in whispered tones if at all—allowing ourselves to release reality and accept what should or could be. We attach ourselves to the characters as they move about the stage; we focus not only on the words, but also the silence as the stories unfold. In this world, we learn what it means to be marveled by the simplicity of the complicated and the complication of the simplicity. Say, what? Let that sink in.

The most masterful craftsmen learn to appreciate the intricacy required to communicate dramatically the simple things that are really quite deep. Therein lies the first challenge of an **effective** communicator. **We must accept the responsibility of individual expression to educate, entertain, and enhance the lives of those we touch.** In other words, while our story seems simplistic, the preparations are extremely complex. Since even before Shakespeare, thespians (actors) have strived to deliver reality in a make-believe world. Why? We all live in a reality that is rarely duplicated from one to another, while we struggle to understand life's dilemmas that we face together. That is to say…we live in the same house, yet we arrange the decor differently.

On the stage, we find ourselves in the hero, the villain, or maybe the nondescript walk-on character that ties the plot all together. Proper theater is exhausting not just for the players, but for those who dare to live through it. **Bring the logic of the stage to your presentations, pitches**

and life to discover the magic available through its connection to reality. Shakespeare said it first and perhaps best in his play, *As You Like It*: "All the world's a stage, and all the men and women merely players." We live on a stage. We do this with ever-evolving plots and subplots. You are the star, the producer, and director of this show called "Life!" Are you seizing the opportunity to expose your reality in an effort to advance your mission?

Radio

As with most creative distribution points, there is no absolute date for the origination of this medium. As a matter of fact, it is tough to nail down its inventor and creator. Some say Marconi; others say Fessenden; and even others reply it was some guy looking to cut a record deal. Regardless of the inventor, the journey began in the late 1800s and continues to evolve today. This, to me, is the most creative medium available as it requires a dying sense to be experienced fully—**imagination**.

In its beginnings, families would sit by its glow and allow their minds to roam to worlds unknown. Listeners could stand beside the batter at home plate, feel the crack of the bat, experience the eruption of the crowd, and, finally, jog alongside

Babe Ruth around the bases. Please note, they would **allow** their minds to roam. Imagination, while natural, is something that we must give permission to move freely.

From westerns to mysteries to suspense and science fiction, and even today, when used properly, the reality of sound and inflection continues to captivate. This was the tool used in 1938 by Orson Welles (You young guys look him up.) when he created a masterful product, "War of the Worlds." This program used the medium so well that, literally, thousands of people thought planet Earth was being invaded by visitors from outer space! It's amazing what the mind can allow to live if we plant the seeds and fertilize properly.

The challenge in today's visually-saturated market is that we seem to be losing this creative ability of imagination because *we want to see it*. A good communicator can still dramatize to the point that the audience will individually see past what is known to what seems real as perception allows. (I'll provide more on this, in detail, as we go along. Keep your ears open! You never know what you might *see*.)

While we have captioned this as radio, the logic is applied to all manners of audio delivery.

Cinema (Movies)

Another enigma, as it is also difficult to nail down, is the originator of motion pictures. The first moving picture camera hit the scene in the late 1800s, but the content was limited in time, scope, and relevance. More of a "Wow" moment than a "Whoa" event, "Hmm" seems a similar reaction to some content making the rounds today. I digress. In the mid-1920s, sound was introduced to film. The talkies brought dialogue, soundtracks, and immersion into creativity only previously imagined.

No matter the timeline, lives were forever changed with this creation, and we continue to sit in awe of the amazing people who weave the stories of our lives on the big screen. In the world of communication, there is little that surpasses the majesty of the opening shot and the ability of celluloid to catapult us into a world or worlds never previously known. Sitting in a dark room with a screen larger than life immersed in surrounding sounds, music, and dialogue, we can and often do allow ourselves to be moved by this art. Walking away with more than just a story, we depart with an alteration to our logic and understanding, hopefully, in a good way. Thanks to films' ability to stretch our **imagination** by allowing us a front row seat to the drama and adventures of life we shape an alternative reality resulting from greater communicative freedom.

Television

Invented in the late 1920s and mass produced by the 1940s, this electronic box that now hangs on the wall, rides on an arm, or is available in a vast array of configurations continues to impact communication. Taking the techniques of stage and movies in combination with the sounds of radio, this marvel entertains, educates, and informs. Once a rare luxury, television or TV is now considered a necessity in homes around the world, for news, information, and varied programming delivered to a wide variety of demographic targets. Similar to its electronic cousins, this canvas offers instructions to communicators in ways to mesmerize while masterfully relaying information and entertaining.

No longer is it four channels with foil on the antenna. Instead, we can enjoy 400 channels in 6.1 separation surround sound exploding off the screen and impacting every life. This "idiot box," as some have named it, provides more than a tune-in, zone-out reality. On the contrary, the **ingenuity** of this media provides an interactive avenue to grow and revel in strong storytelling that will outlive us all. Television, unlike all before, is a communal way of communicating. It allows us to watch and share our perspectives on the content as it rolls by. Thanks to technology, we also have the digital video recorder (DVR) that allows us to pause and discuss or to answer that ever-plaguing question, "What did he say?"

So, just what in the world does all this unrelated media mumbo jumbo have to do with communication? Uhh....everything! In today's tech society, the deluge of information has played right into the hands of communicators. Presenting information in a style that recognizes the preferred communication modes of the attendees allows you to speak AND be heard, enthralling an audience in time-tested ways that are rapidly becoming the norm.

Should you be tempted to use actual audio, video clips, or other materials to enhance your presentation, be aware of copyright laws and use restrictions. When in doubt, leave it out or perhaps be hit with a lawsuit. A tough and costly lesson it can be as I have regrettably had to learn repeatedly.

From the stage we experience the **intimacy**

of information.

From radio, we gain the power of sound and the **impact** provided.

Cinema provides knowledge of grandeur and promotes **imagination**.

From TV, we see the **ingenuity** of reducing it all to a personal level providing insight and individual involvement.

Intimate...impact...imagination...ingenuity. The *I's* have it. Now let's get down to the implementation!

Chapter 2 – Words

Before we can begin any effective dialogue concerning use of the spoken language, please understand this basic truth: **Your words will always precede you.** Be it an email, a resume, a query letter, or a text, your words go before you! Make them count and count them up. Should your journey begin with a conversation, your conversation is what? Words! In the latter, you have the luxury of other great communicative tools, such as inflection, emphasis, and dialect, not found in the written. More on all of the above as we press on. But first let's do the math.

According to people much smarter than me, there are over one million words in the English language. These experts deduce that approximately 300,000 refer to technical verbiage and scientific jargon leaving an estimated 700,000 words for you and me to tote around and use.

It is not likely that you access nearly three quarters of a million words regularly, so the experts continued to deduce that the average human has about 10,000 stored on their hard drive (brain) with daily utilization of around 5,000 words. Talk about time on their hands! But thanks to their calculations and diligence, we discover our first obstacle in great communications—finding the right words at the right time for the right audience with the right meaning. And you thought you were just talking.

Please understand that I am not, nor do I claim to be a grammatical example to be held in high regard among the learned. I have often subscribed to the theory that all you need are periods, commas, question marks, and exclamation points. Colons, semi-colons and ellipses are for showoffs (just kidding), even though I will drop one in from time to time to have my editor say I used it wrong. Or is it the usage that was in error? I never seem to get that. However, in my years of working with writers, directors, and talent, I have been able to squeeze out some logic of the power of what is written, spoken or displayed. So, while this is not a chapter on punctuation (which is important and why great communicators have great editors), it is one of power and emphasis. Say, what?

Good versus great! When we take the value of words and their involvement in communication, we land in two primary camps. The first is that of the worker, the one who realizes in order to convey effective information, fundamental knowledge is required. This person will delve into data, examine the potential, arrange the outline, and present to the audience. They know the value of words and are very selective in the process and implementation. This is a good communicator with value and not to be slighted in any way. They are buttoned up with facts and figures and present the same in a professional way hoping half the audience stays awake and walks away with some valued information.

Then there is the craftsman! This is the one who has seen the value of the research and knowledge but takes it to another level. This is where methodology meets message, message meets needs, and needs meets results; you get the idea. Let's look a little closer at this in-demand and successful communicator and what makes him or her so.

Research – The wordsmith does not settle on standardized data as it relates to their mission. While they are interested in the fundamentals, such as age, gender, income and aspirations of their audience, they go a little deeper. They ask questions like:

- What drives them?
- How is my content relevant to their lives?
- How do they define success, happiness, and fulfillment?

This is the foundation that will allow for not just a more meaningful presentation but a more involved audience with interest. The two basic questions that must be answered in your research phase are:

- Who are you talking to?
- Why should they listen?

Important, yet obvious, this info will vary from conversation to conversation even when the topic is the same. Different targets require differing logic and style. If you are saying, "This is beginning to sound like it requires effort," you are right. Be thankful for search engines that allow you to delve deep with far less time than your predecessors.

Evaluate – Here's another frightening word. When we begin to evaluate the relevance of our info, oftentimes, we are driven out of our comfort levels and forced to think like someone else. This is what *creative* types call getting out of the box. This is important, but always remember you must examine the contents of the box prior to exiting because inside you'll find the foundation of your building (more on that later). With evaluation of your audience and material, you become aware of common traits allowing you to streamline your delivery to fit the need.

Remember that media content from before? This is where we first apply that wisdom. Are you talking to geeks or freaks? I mean that in a good way. In this instance, a freak would be a person with minimal understanding of complicated data you are delivering. Geeks…well, you get it. Demographically, whom are you addressing?

A 50-year-old geek may seem more like a freak while a 20-year-old freak may have the depth of a geek. True, it's all perception. An educated guess is mandatory, however, if you hope to have impact. Stage, screen, radio, or idiot box—how will your audience, for the most part, accept your credibility while supporting your information?

What's the *leave behind*?

    Listen – It just seems to be getting tougher. I thought I was here to speak. True. Before you speak, you would be wise to listen. Note the following definition according to www.dictionary.com, (emphasis, mine):

> lis·ten [**lis**-*uh*n]
> ### *verb (used without object)*
> 1.   To give **attention** with the ear; attend closely for the purpose of **hearing**; give ear.
> 2.   To pay attention; **heed**; obey

    We're unpacking now! Did you catch that "listen" is a verb, meaning there is action associated with it? The listener must be involved with the content being projected. Giving **attention** means analyzing the information. **Hearing** implies allowing the material to go past the superficial "Uh huh" and into the "I see." Yes, you can see with your ears. Once we have paid attention and heard the interest of those we are about to address, the **heed** should come natural because, once the demand is realized, we are on the way to meet it. But how can I listen to an audience when I'm presenting and have never spent time with them?

Thanks for asking, we're back to that listening with your eyes! Say, what?

By noting audience reactions to your words, you will hear loud and clear if your ship is on course. Perhaps even more importantly, before you speak, take a moment to peruse the crowd to hear what they are saying with their eyes. You will find some hungry for information, others there because their boss made them come, still more looking for a "day away" and, finally, the "I was told there was a buffet" group. So feed them. It is very important to identify perceived supporters and opponents...as well as provide fresh pastries.

Assemble – Now we have arrived at *the box*—the place everyone says we must get out of. I concur that exiting from the confines of formulaic new speak is a must. Please understand that, prior to exiting, there is data inside that package you will need to examine. Fundamentally speaking, the five W's are essential to the building of effective communications. Before you begin any presentation, it is imperative to record this data and stay on task. Wandering off this path can, and often does, result in failure to communicate.

Inside this box you may not find all of the above, nor are they all mandatory. But, before you jump and become the creative wizard, decide the need for each and build them in.

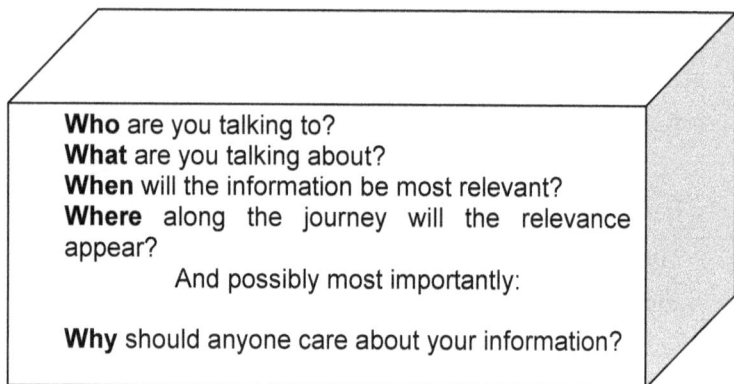

> **Who** are you talking to?
> **What** are you talking about?
> **When** will the information be most relevant?
> **Where** along the journey will the relevance appear?
>   And possibly most importantly:
>
> **Why** should anyone care about your information?

Translate – This next-to-the-last step is critical in preparing for a meaningful presentation, speech, sales pitch, or just a basic conversation. Translation is the seam, if you will, of all who would speak. Supplied with the data above, you are ready to make relatable connections to your audience. Take the knowledge of their complicated lives and the intertwining of friends, jobs, home, travel, needs, wants, and dreams, and begin to weave your message accordingly. Again, your subject matter may not have deliverables in all of their translation points—but those that are there should be addressed. While you may be presenting information relevant to a business goal, most audiences are translating to a personal level to provide clarity and relevance.

And finally...

Emote – It's show time! You are ready to *mean it like you say it*. Digging into those 5,000 words you have so readily available, it's time to let the power flow. Grab some verbs to accent the nouns while the adjectives paint the picture, and drive your vision home to an audience ready to receive. Here's a couple of points to ponder at this point:

> **1.** Words have power; use them! Never allow them to use you!

By this, I mean when in doubt, leave it out. Know when to stop your elaboration, should you note unexpected reactions. Watch the crowd, take your cues, and be prepared to shift at a moment's notice. While you never intend to offend, beware the pitfalls of humor and life comments to a diverse audience. A laugh or point is only valid when appreciated universally.

Most importantly, mind your brain power when talking to those not equipped to match wits. For example, a college professor speaking to a crowd of high school kids and their parents should mind their circuitous meandering to an impervious locale never intended for the inappropriate participants. What? Never take the long way to a destination best described with minimizations. Minimize to maximize! Your intellect, while admirable, can alienate if the audience needs a thesaurus to follow. Next:

    2.   Avoid absolutes, absolutely.

Let's be honest. Is there really a *best* anything? Can there be a true *one-time offer*? Today's audience has heard it all, seen it all, and lined their bird cages with your analytics. This crowd wants the facts as you know them. They will make the decision as the *best* in their world.

Exception, absolutes are valid as long as they are substantiated by the individual.

    ✓   *All our dreams can come true, if we have the courage to pursue them.*

                              Walt Disney

When an absolute places the power on the individual for fulfillment, it becomes valid. Words like, **our** and **can** with **if** and **we** provide support to the individual effort required for fulfillment. It's up to you to find a personal greatest and achieve self-defined success! Say, what? You define your personal absolutes as you are the only one qualified to do so. As a way of recall to the basics, note the acronym:

- Research
- Evaluate
- Listen
- Assemble
- Translate
- Emote

Effective communication revolves around the ability to **RELATE** to an audience as individuals not en masse. When you take the time to do the homework, the results will take you home.

> ✓ It's less about what you **say** and more about what they **hear!**

Before we leave the world of words, hear this: Beware the bridge! In communication, that is a tick used to attempt to transition point to point. For example, the constant utterance of "Uh." Listen: "Uh" is not a communicative operative! The most overused word, "Uh," in most presentations, uh, is in reality an obvious, uh, sign that you, uh, are, uh...unprepared. I have witnessed many speeches, orations, presentations and elaborations that have had their effectiveness diminished by "Uh." If you, from time to time, need time to gather your thoughts, as we all do, use one of the most underutilized techniques—Silence. Right, say nothing. Take a moment, collect your thoughts, breathe, and watch for reactions. Silence used correctly provides great dramatic impact. So, no more "Uh," "Duh!" or other bridges that are often washouts:

- I know, right?
- You follow?
- You hear me?
- With me?
- Really?
- Okay

What's yours? Name it, shame it, and never reclaim it! You hear me, right? I mean, you are with me, really, okay! Uh, anyhow....

Let's focus on three other points to ponder before we press on. Rarely, do I use absolutes, as noted before, but in this case, we are really close. There are three things that guide most of our decisions, declarations, and delusions.

1.   Perspective – *The state of one's
     ideas, the facts known to one

This is the place where we stand that
provides relevance to what we see and determines
what we think. All data received is processed
through this portal, and all known logic is weighed
against our value system to determine how much
we will retain or what will be disregarded. One
person's poverty is another one's plenty. Therein
lies wisdom. **Never underestimate the value of
knowing where your data falls in regard to the
individuals' views.** When at all possible, stand in
their place to weigh the outcome.

2.   Opinion – *A belief or judgment that
     rests on grounds insufficient to
     produce complete certainty

Whoa! Insufficient grounds to produce
certainty! Yet, more than perspective, this is often
the measure of truth as it relates to the individual. I
think I know what I believe but I believe I know
what I think. Say, what? To many, it is more
important to have a thought because it will become
our belief and, once established, it is difficult to
shake it. As my father used to say, "Opinions are
like elbows; most people have a couple." We all

have them and, when used properly, are of extreme relevance. But, turned the wrong way, they are the source of great pain.

3.   Personality – *The visible aspect of one's character as it impresses others

*source...dictionary.com

While perspective and opinion belong to you, your personality is decided upon by others based on your delivery of the other two. Who you are is not always who you think as you stand too close to the source. As I have told many broadcast talent through the years, you can't use the product as the listener since you are the performer. Therefore, we are misguided when listening to ourselves as opposed to listening to the listener. Say, what?

Pay attention. The audience will tell you who you are.

- **Perspective**- How you see
- **O**pinion- How you think
- **Personality**- How you're seen

The **POP** principle is another acronym that

reminds us of communicative fundamentals to shape what we say into who we are.

Note on **POP:** Your physicality, background, credits, and demeanor will factor into the initial reception. He's tall, she's short...kind of stout, awful thin. However, most of those perceived notions will fade once you begin your presentation. While it's important to look the part, it's vital to know the part. Say, what? **Your credibility rests on what you know and how you share it.** So, look as nice as possible, but present with confidence.

Chapter 3 – Styles

Now that you have done your due diligence, you are ready to assemble your information in a style that meets the needs first of the product or service (brand) you are representing to the audience you are addressing.

First truth: Content is King!

Your obligation to your company, your client, and, most importantly, to yourself is to be fully aware of the product or service you represent—to know the advantages, the value, and the credibility the brand holds. To effectively communicate, you **must** operate in truth, factually promoting worth. Awareness of limitations is also important as this is data not often revealed but appreciated when acknowledged. Knowing what you are is important knowing what you are not, just as crucial.

This is where some teams I have worked with fall away. They see their job as a means to an end, not a contribution to a better life for those in the audience. I have heard comments like, "I am selling cable TV, not affecting lives." Really? Consider this thought, if you are a content provider in the entertainment world. Everyone works hard fulfilling, feeding, clothing, housing, and maintaining a semblance of sanity in their household. Your product may be the only respite from a hectic life for a busy family.

For many, the few moments spent around that glowing tube in the evening and weekend are not necessarily efforts to tune out. Perhaps, it is family time to tune in and discuss what is seen as it relates to their private lives. We all have our favorite shows, characters, and news sources. You, TV outlet salesperson, provide that escape and rejuvenation. It is good to know that your product is there dependably at the end of a crazy day. Now, what are you selling? Perhaps it is the opportunity for a consumer to catch their breath and prepare for another day.

One great story I have comes from an interview with a pretty famous guy, whom I can't say by name, as he did not give me permission to use it. But, the story is too good to let rest alone with me. This individual was explaining the need to be aware of the value in us all. The story goes, what happens if I, (the star), wake up in the morning to a toilet that is overflowing, what do I do? Sing to it? No! I call a plumber, a person who has the ability to remedy the situation. The illustration continued that, while on stage, the accolades and applause are directed to the performer. In life, however, often the true stars are the ones who provide a service allowing us to live in peace and take the bows. Wow, wisdom from a rock star!

You alone define the content that will drive relevance and relatable information. Always be over-analytical as to the service or product you provide, and you should find value previously overlooked or over glamorization that could greatly impact credibility negatively.

Second Truth: If content is King, packaging is Queen!

Often referred to as technique, packaging is the varied delivery methods used for impact. Personal analogy: My mother loved Christmas. She loved the lights, the sounds, the peace, and the momentary joy seemingly enjoyed by all. From Thanksgiving to mid- January, our house was adorned with decorations from nativity scenes to Santa. Always at the center of the room was the tree. From my childhood, I remember it was always a real tree to provide scents of the season adorned with enough ornaments and lights that we were often afraid planes would try to land in our yard from the illumination. Underneath rested a virtual sea of gifts—a selection so wide it would often reach from the family room to the breakfast area due to volume. I told you, she loved Christmas!

Each package was adorned in colorful paper, foil, bows, and often hand-written notes. Now, my family was not successful monetarily, even though during the holidays, it seemed we were the richest around. You see, my mom knew the value of brand, image, and packaging. With the brand, Christmas, being supported by the image— giving—the target was more involved and appreciative. Thus, these traditions continued to grow each year with the survivors of the vision. Now, for the record, it was not about content. You may find a single sock in one package and the other would surface much later in another. Providing that much desired anticipation as the quest continued. The material inside mattered less than the excitement of the moment and knowing inside something for you was waiting. Relevance?

> **Anticipation is heightened with proper packaging and audience awareness.**

This leads us to methodology.

Methods of communication are endless. Because your attention span and my wisdom is limited, I will focus primarily on four fundamentals, as most seem to flow from these.

- Straight Ahead
- Journalistic
- Lifestyle
- Humor

Prior to preparation, ponder the style that will, likely, resonate your message with your audience. Taking note of content, relevance, attendees in regard to generational differences, demographics, and mission.

First comes data that falls into the *Dragnet* approach, or straight-ahead method. For those of you too young to remember the amazing Jack Webb and the 1950s TV series, he was a "Just the facts, ma'am" kind of cop. Though he was never much on developing relationships, he could solve any case with simple basic information. This style in your world should only be used when numbers are relevant but not earth shattering.

"There are an estimated 45,000 residents in the target demographic with a noted 3 percent growth rate per year."

Relevant data is best left to handouts or displayed on-screen as its relevance will be noted as you move forward.

Straight ahead...say it!

When the facts meet elaboration requirements, we enter the Journalistic method. This content is delivered factually with more background to provide clarity as to their necessity. Unlike today's journalists, this information should be factual with little slant on its meaning.

"Of the 45,000 noted, it is recommended we remember that 24 percent are new residents who have limited familiarity with our brand."

It is important that our audience is aware that numbers are often slanted but not over-colorized to increase or decrease relevance. That will be discussed later in the POP factor.

As noted in our analogy above, this basic background is similar to those individually-wrapped socks. Our next two are the wrapping that entices us to want to make sure they match.

Journalistic....report it!

Now, we have arrived where communication meets relevance—lifestyle. This is where your previous work begins to reap dividends. This is where you make eye contact and connect in ways that matter. What do the numbers mean to you? How are they important to your family? Your standard of living? Why should you even care?

> "While thinking of those 45,000 we mentioned earlier, remember you were once one of those. Before, you found the value in the brand that is equally concerned in community relations as well as product movement."

It is very important before you journey down this path that you make sure the claims made are substantiated. Fool me once, it's on you; fool me twice, it's on me. Few get a second chance.

This methodology is where the heart of your presentation should live. This is where your logic meets need—where you show me not what's in it for you, but what's in it for us.

Lifestyle...live it!

Finally, and to be used only when absolutely effective, let's talk about the Humor method! We all love to laugh, and there are those who even purport that laughing promotes health. This is where RELATE training, discussed in Chapter Two, comes fully into play. Remember, most humor is at someone or something's expense. What you mean for chuckles could result in listeners mentally exiting. Again, I reiterate: "When in doubt, leave it out."

Humor...laugh about it.

Great presentations, conversations or gatherings will often contain elements from all of the above. The challenge for you is to communicate the relevant information in a way that is informative, entertaining, educational, and impactful, all while sounding real.

Easy, right? IT can be, as long as you focus on the fundamentals, and remember above all, **IT** matters!

Chapter 4 – Tools

I love technology! To the point of near ridiculousness, I possess or long to possess the gadgets, the gizmos, the doodads and anything else that lights up, spews data, or emits a blue light of entertainment. In my home, you will find five flat-screen TVs, three desktop computers, one laptop, two tablets, three smart phones, and a varied collection of must-have tech gear that is either now out of date or in need of updates. By the way, this home is inhabited only by myself and my wife, whom I love. Before you go off on your rants of excess, take your own inventory. All of the above, while excessive perhaps, are tools to be used in ways to more effectively mine data, assemble information, or be entertained. How often do we all fall victim to screen relationships that minimize communication essentials? These are tools that, when taken to the extreme, will sacrifice us at the altar of technology. But, when used effectively, they can lead us into a greater realm of connection.

The next time you are in a public place, note the faces on each other versus the faces on the glowing phones. Technology is our friend and ally that can rapidly become our foe when we forget that we live in relational society. Take a moment to put down the device and look at someone when you converse. It may seem odd at first but, in time, you just might enjoy it. Plus, you can catch that broccoli on your teeth before the boss does. The challenge is to use technology as intended while avoiding the alienation factor.

Therein lies the opportunity to excel for all who speak to groups of one or one million—knowing what to say, how to say it, and delivering in a way that holds up. I'm talking about face-to-face dialogue that provides what tech cannot: personality and interest. While our gadgets provide access to knowledge, we have a secondary source of hardware necessary. Let's open the personal tool box and have a peek at what's available.

42 Say, What?

The first thing we see is…a mirror! Hmm, that seems odd. How can this be of any use to a communicator? Take a look. What do you see? Myself, of course. Indeed, it's you. That is the face that your audience will note, but not just your beauty or rugged handsomeness; those are options. Instead, take a look at the factory basics installed on all models. Just south of the nose and north of the chin lies the portal to verbal expression. From this outlet not only does the information flow, but also expressiveness that can seal a deal, heal a heart, or impart wisdom. This is revealed all from the upturn with teeth for joy, excitement, or affirmation to the downspin for sorrow, disappointment, disillusionment, or discontent. That, by the way, is called your mouth, fundamental to all, but universally varied. All of the above sources of communication from this orifice are made before you speak a word. **Expression is the driver behind anticipation and the forerunner of information.**

Heading north, we note the device provided to not only receive and relay oxygen to the lungs but also the receiver of communication via strong sense (play on words intended). With a crunch, a wiggle, or a flare of this apparatus, your audience is aware that something is very sweet or just not right.

Though "smell-avision" is not a must-have tech gadget yet, you can still convey a sweet aroma with the right use of this standard tool. This would be your nose and the inflection it offers.

Still heading north, we find perhaps our most important instruments of the manufacturer's communiqué gear. So important, they usually travel in pairs and are constant sources of information, frustration, and elaboration. When open wide, they speak excitement, fear, joy, or anticipation. Slivering into almost disappearance allows for suspicion, confusion, or dismay. Spend an extra moment peering into these portals. How long can you hold the gaze without reaction? Probably, not very long, as this is where nothing successfully hides. Windows to the soul? I don't know. It's worth spending time developing in an effort to attain genuineness, sincerity, and believability. These are eyes, peepers, or pools of passion depending upon your upbringing.

Note: These can also be a great source of distraction in relaying information. From our peripheral vision, we may perceive movement as reactionary even when it is not meant to be. Never allow your perception of reactions to justify shifting course in your speech unless absolutely necessary. Know what you know—not what you think shows.

44 Say, What?

Finally, your eyes often function best when they are closed. Say, what? Have you ever noticed when singers hit the high note, the *shades* are down? When deep in conversation, the speaker's lids lay shut? These momentary stretches of darkness provide clarity and are a great tool. However, use sparingly as distractions are often looming in the shadows. Plus, too long in the shadows and slumber may find you.

Just a notch north of said vision devices lies thin strands of hair adorned on ridges used to emphasize the intent of the eyes. We call these eyebrows. Cocking one or raising together can provide impact not available through any other means. Power lives here!

These are just the first tools found inside the box. Like the Swiss Army knife full of attachments, they are the most unknowingly utilized and often under-exercised tool. It's never enough to just know what something is. It is just as important to know what something does and how to use it. A saw in the hands of a novice often incurs injury not only to a project, but also to the user. While in the hands of an expert, using a saw can result in art.

While the face is the operative feature most widely observed, it is important to remember that

great communication is a full-body activity. Proper
exclamations noted with a shrug, extended arms,
hand waves, leg motions, and torso twists all play
into the physicality of making your point. **Use your
body to say what no words can!** That said, never
overuse body motions. Movement is for accent,
not the heart of the matter. Avoid the crutch of
movement as if often appears to be nervousness.

On that subject, as we look into our kit, we
find what we already knew would be there—words!
There is no need to belabor the points made earlier
about the voluminous selections of literary content
at your disposal. (Was that overkill?) Instead, let's
talk about putting them to work.

You are the speaker. Let the words do the
heavy lifting. You just serve them up. In other
WORDS, inflection and intent are indispensable. I
know you think you know what you said but I'm
not sure you said what you think? Say, what?
Translation: Listen to yourself! There is strength in
allowing power words to carry more weight, but
only if you supply the emphasis.

> **Example:** "The chances of success are
> increased only by the desire of those
> seeking it."

Now, here is the same sentence, given
power via emphasis:

Example: "The **chances** of success are
increased only by the **desire** of
those **seeking** it".

By giving inflection to the words in bold
with sincerity, volume, or position, we have
promoted ownership of the mission of success to
the one who is seeking it. Success is not benign; it
must be owned, sought, and nurtured.

Before you present, ALWAYS, proof your
content for words of power and allow the words to
take control. Then, take your mirror and deliver
them out loud to yourself to allow them to take
root.

While on the subject of words, know this
phrase that pays: "reactive phraseology." What
"Amen" is to the preacher, applause to the artist,
and laughter to the funny man, "reactive
phraseology," or "RP" going forward, is to the
communicator.

The mission of most who stand before an
audience to impart perceived wisdom is to have
some sign that points are made, received, and
appreciated. The most widely-used reactive phrases

are "Hello there" or "Good morning." When confronted with these salutations individually or en masse, it is customary to respond with the same, "Good morning" or "Hey" is often the reaction noted. That is acknowledgement, professionalism, and proof that the audience is aware.

I realize that saying "Good morning" repeatedly will result in unusual stares but also can cause special friends to escort you away for a *nice rest*. To avoid that embarrassment, developing your own RPs is advisable.

Rules of the game:

- RP must be true or at least perceived as true
- RP must be connected to the subject (product)
- RP must make sense
- RP must cross socio-economic and cultural lines
- RP should be contagious

When we apply the above criteria to "Good morning," they all fit neatly into the rules noted and really cannot be argued on any level as being irrelevant to the masses. An individual may be having a bad morning but will probably not permit that to alter their response. They are reacting to a source as a courtesy and, unbeknown to them, allowing a truth to take root.

The development of an RP can come from a company logo, a personal commitment, or just a sentiment shared. Regardless of origin, consistency is key. For example, those who know me personally know that I hold my family very dear. They also know of my devotion to the crazy lady who had the nerve to say "Yes" to me many decades ago and become my wife. Now, she is an integral part of my RP collection. When talking with friends or colleagues about my wife, it is most always followed with "whom I love." Therefore, when I say "my wife" in those settings, often I am deluged with the response, "whom you love." It feels good to know that a truth I hold is now held by others as well. The same case applies in all prospects, personal or business.

- "(Your company name here), the leader in broadcast service"
- "(Product), number one in customer satisfaction"
- "(Destination), where love meets life"

You get the idea. The catch is, every time you mention the parenthetical, you include the RP.

I know, it seems redundant and irritating; your audience, however, is not only more likely to remember it but, before the end, many will be quoting it before you do. Placement is vital, thus, bringing us to our next tool.

Rehearsal involves acting to anticipate the reaction which will garner the greatest reaction from those you hope to impact. Say, what? That is to say, be prepared to prepare.

As with any tool, the proper environment will provide the greatest result. For instance, using that circular saw mentioned before in the middle of a dining room during your Thanksgiving dinner to carve the turkey may find you on the tray with the fowl you intended to serve. However, using said saw in a workshop on the Monday prior to Turkey Day to ensure all have a place to sit will may make you a hero. It is the same with rehearsal. Long before you step on the stage, enter the conference room, or set up your e-meeting, find your sanctuary and prepare.

When I say sanctuary I am not referring to a church or other place of worship. Instead, this is your high holy place—a place of solitude away from all that would distract. It is a locale where you compile your thoughts, arrange the meanings, and elaborate internally on the outcome you hope for.

For me, it's my morning walk in the heat of a Texas summer that provides inspiration. Wandering about the walking trail in my neighborhood allows me to reflect, reject, and respond to the audience of one—me. With my Bluetooth recorder in my pocket and microphone around my ear, I am able to open up and begin the journey.

Granted, this allows for some great stares and chuckles from my fellow sojourners. When I furrow my brow and point to my earpiece though, their stares dissolve. Bluetooth is a blessing and a curse. Before its arrival, we could spot the crazy people. They were the ones talking to themselves. Now, you never know who might be listening or if it's just voices in their heads. Regardless, leave them be. The crazy ones and the *important ones* should always be left alone. This gives credence to the adage, "There is a fine line between a genius and an idiot." At varied points in our lives, we all play the role of each, I fear. Pardon my digression.

The point is, find your spot. Your isolation place. Your refuge. Then, listen to yourself objectively. This is Round One. Round Two is to find a source you trust to tell you the truth and rehearse again in an audience of two, preferably neither of which is a family member or close friend. The reaction of the latter usually falls into one of two camps: 1) "Oh, I could listen to you read the phone book" (Fan camp) or 2) "You get paid to do this?" (Foe camp). Neither is productive.

Find a mentor, trusted colleague, or a waitress at the lunch counter who will give you honest feedback. Before you go, you need to know! It is not necessary nor recommended that you present your content in totality to your *audience*, rather, only that your data is discussed. Trust me, by the time you get to the meeting or presentation, you will have decided to make some changes. In other words, be prepared to be unprepared.

Chapter 5 – Drama

Now we move into the minute details of great communication by recognizing the need for dramatic intent. As noted earlier, Shakespeare said, "All the world's a stage, and all the men and women merely players." Regardless of the advances in technology and our ability to under communicate, this truth stands firm. **Life is drama, and great communication demands it.** When I get to this portion of live training, I am often greeted with, "I'm no actor." First of all, yes you are. If you live on Earth, you are involved in acting every day. Next, drama is not acting...acting is drama. Say, what?

Please understand that the following information will not, and is not intended to, aid you in developing acting skills. Instead, the hope is that you will become more aware of the fundamentals of the art you express every day. In the process, it is desired that, as you explore the relevance of drama in all lives, you will better relate to others.

In conversations with actors and directors over the years, I have heard one phrase repeatedly, "Acting is reacting." Truth! All great actors understand that their craft is formed in the backstory that allows for elaboration in story development. Along that same path, hear this, "Communication is reactionary interaction." Say, what? We react in a way to invite interaction from all involved. When interaction occurs, success is usually a result.

How so? Before we speak, we see. As we discussed previously, great communicators are great listeners, not only hearing but heeding information given. Taking that to the dramatic level, great communicators have great vision. While we can see with our ears, we can also hear with our eyes. Now, this is just getting weird! You haven't seen or heard anything yet.

As a child, I recall my mother often saying, "Look at me," when she felt I was being perhaps a little less than forthcoming. The same rings true in all communications. Eye to eye is one of the toughest tests. The challenge is to look into the eyes of the one speaking to you AND allow them to look into yours. The eyes, some say, are the windows to the soul. Also, they are the portals to the truth. While we may not be hiding anything, it often appears we just might be when we cannot comfortably look into someone's eyes while, simultaneously, allowing them to peer back into ours.

To hone this, let's go back to the tool kit for a daily exercise. For at least a minute a day, get your face in front of a mirror and make eye contact with yourself. Hold the pose as long as you can without changing expression. Never before has 60 seconds drug on so long. Next, while still in front of the mirror, spend another minute exercising interaction reactions. This is not an exercise in pretention, but instead a reality check of how you relate and interact.

Think of instances of joy and note your reaction. Think also of assorted emotions that we cannot hide—frustration, anger, and others. It is very important that you are not faking it. Allow yourself to be genuinely impacted to provide for greater emotional connection. It can be difficult for some serious leaders to participate in this exercise, but the successful ones see the value. We are all more than meets the eye; however, this is where our impressions of one another take root.

Other ways in which the eyes reveal intent is in physicality. I am not, nor will I ever be, an expert in reading body language. There are volumes written on this topic and most are excellent reads. On the other hand, I have become rather gifted in the area of body *punctuation*. Oh yeah, it's real. Be aware of your audience's involuntary movements. Watch their hands. Are they tense, tight, or open? Are their shoulders relaxed, strained, or clenched? Their head—does it tilt, shake, or move with certain thoughts? When you combine what you see with what you hear, you are set to live the drama of the moment. Allow for that interactive reaction. Another phrase that pays—be aware!

The most important aspect of the dramatic communicator is, likely, something that cannot be taught, learned, or inherited. **Passion**! Passion takes your objective from *I might* to *I do*; *I could* to *I did*; *I should* to *I will*; and *I would* to *let's go!* It keeps us up at night, gets us on our feet in the morning, and gives value to all we do. It's also the most personal aspect of drama and life. Define it! What burns in you to the point that you can't keep still?

What gives validity to all you are while allowing you to give with all you've got? I see the eyes rolling and the head shakes, "Getting a little sappy, here, right?" Not at all.

Your passion will inhabit all you do and help make you all you desire to be. Note, I did not say all you could be; other ingredients later will deliver on that. Passion is internal, driving the success that is external. It is important to know passion is not something we make; instead it makes us. Hard fact, if your passion is not driving what you do maybe it's time to do something else. Phrase that pays, let it burn!

Breathe easy. It gets easier, not quite formulaic but, hopefully, easier to rationalize. Whew! As the road to dramatic interpretation continues, comes the most common word heard when talking with dramatists, **Motivation**. I can't think of a time when working on a creative project that the question, "What's the motivation?" hasn't arose. At first, the director in me wants to say the motivation is that often oversized paycheck. But, I have been involved in many volunteer programs where that could not be the case. Or could it?

We often define pay as cash for services rendered when, in fact, a payday could be the expressions left in the wake of a great performance.

Motivation, like passion, is highly personal in nature, yet more definable. For the stage player, motivation can come from the reviews, the applause, and the people hanging by the stage door waiting to thank them for touching their lives. Or, preferably it comes from within. When you have put all you are into a project—be it entertainment, presentation, conversation, or meeting—your motivation is often the exhilaration that precedes and the accolades that follow, both internal and external. While it feels good to have your work acknowledged by the crowds and your peers, there is no greater motivation than the personal awareness that you have left it all on the stage, in the conference room, or over the kitchen table. Motivation is an expected outcome in response to your tireless efforts to understand and deliver. Phrase that pays, let it fly! That is motivation!

While we are engaged in the cerebral process of dramatic development (motivation), next we enter the dream state—the vision of taking what is imagined into development—aided in this step by our divinely appointed mentors. This allows us to begin drawing our outline for personal and group involvement and expectations. For me, my parents would head the list as examples of how to be what you say and expect the same from everyone. Therein lies **inspiration**.

Bill and Ruth McWhorter: he, a career Air Force guy and she, a fourth-grade dropout, were two of the smartest people I've known and a primary source of my inspiration. . First, let's talk about Dad, a man of few words but extreme examples. As mentioned earlier, he was a career military guy. As a matter of fact, until I was 12, I thought my name was "Soldier." I was expected to know my mission and accomplish it to the best of my ability. Dear old Dad would often say, "Before you start up that hill, make sure it's one worth dying on." I was much older until that made sense, but, now I am very selective about the hills I defend or the battles I will fight. The point here is that life is about maintaining control in all circumstances when the outcome matters. These principles inspire the way I live.

Now to mom, the fifth-born child and the baby of the family, she never knew her dad. He departed the day she was born. This left my 4'11" grandmother to raise five kids alone in a time when most families with both parents were struggling. After Mom dropped out in the fourth grade, she worked a cotton farm to help support the family and was never able to return to her education. But, she was wise past academia. I am thankful that I was able to share in her wisdom, and share two pieces with you: "All people are of value and your time with them will add to your worth" and the one that drove me through the years, "As long as you try, no one can call you a failure." More words to live by!

I am reminded often of their control, concern, and compassion along with the understanding that we are all in this together. Let's make it work. That is inspiration that drives my vocation and, my life.

What about you? Perhaps your home life was not filled with uneducated, military-minded philosophers. I have no doubt that if you think about it, you can name many who have gone before and some still hanging around that inspire you to greatness. Name them and allow their examples to lead. Phrase that pays, learn from others!

This brings us to **determination**! Remember when I said earlier, "Avoid absolutes absolutely with few exceptions"? This is one exception: Determination combined with focus is an unstoppable force that will deliver you past any obstacle.

Factors in determining determination:

Destination – We can't get to where we are going unless we know where that is. Before you begin, visualize the conclusion. As I was told once by a very famous author, "Before I begin, I know where I will end." That allows determination to take root as you understand everything builds to the culmination, and until you have arrived you won't rest (hopefully).

Obstacles – Along your path, things will fall out of place and appear to alter the journey. Basically, these fall into two groups: First, real, like running out of money before you get out of the gate; loss of market share or shifts in Area of Dominant Influence (ADI), and demographic relevance. Planning for the known will prepare you for the unexpected. Note, planning is not preparation; it is a cousin of expectation. We expect challenges; how we respond will allow focus. That is where advanced training comes in. We'll get there. But, more crippling than the expected or known obstacles are the ones we create. That is our second group of obstacles. The ones we birth in our mind that can have deep impact. What if no one shows up? What if no one cares? There is already an overcrowded marketplace. How do I compete? And on and on and on. Never allow the mental madness to block your path. Sure, troubles will come, but allow them to organically develop. There is no need to fertilize the negativity. Be prepared to be unprepared. Say, what?

Waypoints – Let me go back to childhood for a moment. I remember very plainly going on vacation with the family. That usually meant off to the grandparents for a week or to visit friends in other states. Those were the destinations. Of even more excitement was wondering where we would stop along the way. How many motels would we visit? Would there be a pool? What about buffets? Perhaps we would visit the dinosaur park, the haunted museum. You get the idea. The final stop is known but, often times, the unknown fuels the determination.

Always allow for rest stops on your journey to provide for reflection, interaction, and personal involvement. As I have aged, it's funny, but I seem to remember the waypoints as well as the final stops. My dad, a military man, remember, was a guy who could drive for 12 to 18 hours straight. "Are we there, yet?" was a phrase we repeated as we never knew if and when we would stop along the way. "Just over the next hill, around the corner, up the street, or in the next town" was the usual response. This provided an often overlooked aspect of communicators, **anticipation.** Provide points of connection in your presentations not anticipated but very much appreciated. Keep it real, relatively speaking.

Detours – The most hated of all road signs are those indicating detours. I can remember the exasperated sighs from the front seat as our well-laid plans were shifted by the errors of others or construction. We were redirected off the main highway to the side streets into the small towns to gaze at people we had no intention of seeing or meeting. On more than one occasion, these unplanned side trips proved more than beneficial. They offered perspective along with wisdom. I recall one such occasion, en route to Kansas City, to visit friends when an accident diverted us into a small town with one stop light and one cafe. Weary from the road, we decided to stop for lunch and to stretch our legs at the single eatery.

As I recall, inside there were maybe 15 tables and only one open. We took it. Our waitress was missing several teeth but was not afraid to offer up a smile and a "How can I help you?" While she served up the cheeseburger plate, I took in the scenery and sat in awe. This was not a blue-collar town; instead it was a no-collar, t-shirt, and overalls kind of gathering. This was the type of place that kids dream of leaving one day and no one would seemingly want to call home intentionally. Or, that was my supposition. Much to my surprise, as I sat and experienced the happiness on the faces, the loud conversations from table to table, not to mention the burger, I found unexpected value.

I found people with minimal means but maximum success. Still, more than 40 years later, I recall this as one of my greatest vacation memories. Listening to the old-timers wax over days gone by and the more to come, I remember thinking as we exited, "It's not where you live that matters; it's who you live with." Be prepared to be bombarded with detours as you present your information. There is wisdom in the audience. Take the time to notice. Somebody lives here!

Alternate ending – Along those lines, be ready to adjust your destination as warranted by reception. Say, what? Being prepared to be unprepared, remember? While you are set to deliver and are the master of your information, your audience reactions, inquiries, or attendance may require a shift. Your points remain valid and your finale remains intact, but the means to the end can shift without notice.

For instance, I was once presenting on a marketing structure for a major film title. My marketing studies showed this movie would benefit greatly from primary broadcast and minimal out-of-home support such as bus backs and billboards. During the presentation, it was noted by a participant that the primary marketing team had assembled an implementation plan, along with scheduling and placement of creative assets outside of broadcast. With this knowledge, my focus shifted to content and relevant support across all electronic, social, network, and satellite media. I made points without distraction by eliminating what had already been said and led deeper discussion on wider disbursement points. This promoted greater dialogue on content. No one was aware of my original intent, and the campaign was a great success. Also, the movie made a ton of money! Just saying.

As noted earlier, none of the qualities mentioned will make you an "actor." However, if you acknowledge their validity in all you know, hopefully, they will dramatically assist you in more effective communication. That is the goal, right?

Chapter 6 – Ends & Odds

Before we wrap up this section on fundamentals, here are some random thoughts that should enhance your next speech, presentation, conversation, or muttering.

If you don't know, let it go.

There was an old commercial years ago that brought focus to claims of quality and relevance to product placement. The slogan was, "Parts is parts," translated to mean we give you what we want, and you call it what you will. Does it really matter? Why...yes, yes it does! You see, facts are facts and must be universally accepted before calling them facts. Say, what?

It's like this. Thinking is not believing, and believing is not knowing. Elaboration: You see, before I would sit on a bar stool, I need to deduce some realities. For example, what type of wood was used to build said stool? Are the dimensions suitable to hold a person of my stature? Once that scenario is satisfied, other considerations can be made. Noting that the third leg is a bit shorter than the other two, for example, may force a belief that weight displacement must be primarily forward to allow stability. Even though I thought through the components and noted the flaw in workmanship, before I sit, I must factor in what I know.

That being said, the law of gravity applies and, if my logic and research is flawed or misplaced, I will fall to the floor resulting in pain, embarrassment, and possible expense. That is knowledge. Knowing there is an outcome based on cause and effect, I can be better prepared to face the scenario and possible outcomes. Did I want a drink that bad? I'll just get it to go.

This is a roundabout way of saying to never let your thoughts or beliefs cloud what you know. That does not mean to do away with doubts—only, identify them accurately at the outset, allowing for judgment to be made based on the data. It's kind of back to that hill you are willing to die on. Facts are facts...thoughts and beliefs, negotiable. When you introduce facts not proven, your credibility takes a major hit. "Here's what I think" covers you and makes you human.

Critics are real...you are one!

Beware the press clippings! You have worked hard, done your due diligence, your research and spent many hours in rehearsal, rewriting, mirror time, and inflection study. Your graphics were amazing, your tone impeccable, your content relatable, and your persona stellar. Shoot, at the end of your presentation, there was applause! I mean people were slapping their hands together for you! Some even stood up. Wow, if only that bully from the fourth grade could see you now. You were a rock star! Hang on, Elvis! Fame is fleeting; success lies in retention.

While you have perhaps touched a few nerves and pointed the team toward a destination, the validity of your oratory prowess comes later. When does it come? 1) When the emails roll in referencing today's gathering; 2) When the words you said take root and provide a launch for those so quick to clap and grab a donut on the way out the door; and 3) When senior management invites you back to speak to the rest of the team. You get the idea. Therein lies results. Now, I am not saying to avoid reveling in the back slaps, the "Way to go" and "Dang, you're good!" comments. Be appreciative and make sure they have your card to check in later with their success stories.

But, what about the ones where the applause is light or nonexistent? What about the ones with benign comments and the exits filled with sighs of relief? "I thought he would never shut up" is the feeling that permeates the hall. What then? Be appreciative and make sure you are available for comments, and learn from it. Learn?

Last week at (company name here), they figuratively carried you off the field on their shoulders and today you feel trampled underfoot. What's the lesson here? Figure out what worked and what didn't. Your content may have resonated with some or even most, but if the "big boss's" response was cool or even tepid, your accolades may fall victim. That is one reason audience awareness is so important. **Knowing who is where and sensing responses can shift delivery style, content, and data.** It's also a great case for not inviting leaders to learn about leading…but that's another book.

So which one matters most? Neither and both. Say, what? The truth is, those who love us are vital to our personal mental manipulation. I mean that in a most positive way. Being mentally aware of our positive traits are how we continue to develop our style and personality. Those who could care less are just as valid. We learn from both audience reactions what to do or what not to do, and a dose of humility will keep us on the path.

There could be another more important root to the issue, though, and worthy of consideration. It is the critic that lives within! You know when you were prepared, you are aware when your content is focused, you have confidence in your presentation and you, without apologies, leave it all on the stage! Aha! There is that passion thing again.

Brevity!

Yes.

But never at the expense of outcome management. Sometimes an apparent over- delivery of information is necessary to provide data for closure. For example, over 30 years ago, my father-in-law was involved in what could have been a pretty major accident with an eighteen-wheeler. The fact that the accident could have occurred is frightening, but, recognizing the surrounding events leading up to it were educational and revealing.

His tale went something like this:

"It was a cool day—you know, the kind of day when the heat has not yet been acquainted deeply with the humidity, leaving the comfort level tolerable without the use of air conditioning. The kind of day when you roll the windows down on the car so the Texas freshness can roll in. That's the day it was. Travelling along Interstate 35 through the concrete canyon of roads, I found myself approaching a large truck hauling fuel. As I pulled up alongside, our speeds were similar and we sailed along side by side for maybe a mile. As we approached the low point of the canyon, I sensed a *tug* on my vehicle and I sensed a sensation of being drawn ever closer to this mighty machine. Immediately, I knew this could get ugly. Realizing I was no longer in control of the vehicle, I released the wheel and watched as I was *pulled* first alongside the truck, then in front of this massive machine. Staring into the grill, my resolve intensified to stay focused and allow the physics to work themselves out. Next, I rounded a corner and found myself heading northbound, clinging to the side of the truck heading southbound. This is where it got really dicey. The driver looked down and saw me! Thankfully, he remained calm and advised me to shift into neutral. I complied. Gradually, he slowed allowing the vortex to maintain and our 'connection' to remain. Eventually, we stopped—he facing south and me facing north—both alive and grateful for an incredible ending."

Now, that is a long story to say, "I was almost killed yesterday afternoon." Could the same info not been reduced to: "Be careful around big trucks; they pull a great force"? Maybe. But, following the art of the story, we learn to be aware of our surroundings in addition to the climate, the speed, and the laws of physics, and to not allow your logic to get lost in your reasoning.

I am a proponent of the Keep It Simple, Stupid (KISS) principle as attention spans of most audiences are limited to the information they find relevant. However, there is much to be said about the MILE principle—Meaningful Information Limits Exasperation. Yeah, I made that up. Outcomes have deeper impact when we understand their origins. The challenge for the communicator is to know when to explain further and when to stop explaining altogether.

Preparedness

We have spent time stressing the significance of being ready, right, and resilient in your due diligence, and also the benefit of study, research, and evaluating all necessary data to effectively present. In doing so, I hope you realize that what you do is not business as usual. Rather, in doing so, you are or should hope to become an artist. You take a blank canvas, then provide a background, foreground, and periphery support to "edu-tain" your audience (education meets entertainment). This is a most admirable profession. Some might even say that it's a calling. Regardless of your descriptor, agree on one point: While there is art to the craft, there is work to the art. Say, what? Nothing important happens by accident. While it may originate on a bar napkin or on a casual walk, a song, story, show, or sales presentation begins at the end with an anticipated conclusion. When one labors intensely, craftsmanship comes alive and meets the goal!

To quote a well-known author, who did not give me permission to quote him, "Creativity is not natural; it's work!" This is a saying that rang true often in my journey when hiring writers, actors, and other creative types on more than one occasion talking to aspiring artists fresh out of college looking for their *break*. They would interview well, carry themselves properly, and were even careful with their social network image. Then came the big request from me, "Send me your portfolio for review." Brows would furrow and lips clinch. "Portfolio? My ideas are in my head. I just need a corridor to express them." "Aha...so you are a dreamer?" I said. "Let's make another appointment when you are a doer, and we will dream together." This seems harsh and the phraseology was varied depending upon the climate of conversation. But, the world of art has enough dreamers. The craft becomes your profession only when you do the work.

Let them read...

Thanks to technology, persons who present have a vast array of tools to help develop impact instantaneously. One such tool is presentation software—pretty slides, video, audio, and enhancements to meet every sense. When used properly, they can become your signature to seal the deal. When used improperly, they become your crutch.

When creating your *show,* be careful to never insult your audience's mental abilities. For the most part, THEY CAN READ. When we read a slide word for word to an audience, their eyes may start to glaze over and daydreaming begins. Using bullet points on-screen and necessary data from your face should engage the audience to interact and become physically and mentally involved. Encouraging them to take notes promotes comprehension beyond your narrative on what they can read on the screen. If you still feel your information is important enough to be quoted properly, show the key points on the slides after the dialogue addressing them in summary. Technology is great as long as it is used properly.

Leave Behinds

Leaving it all on stage, in the conference room, or on a web chat is the nucleus that what you *leave behind* is a developmental tool. Make sure that you reward attendees whenever possible with materials to support your messaging. This can be as simple as a copy of your outline or presentation or as complex as an additional training video and book. Note: This is for contracted training, not for every breakfast, lunch, or dinner you address. Additionally, when speaking before a group during a meal, I find it best to restrain from eating until my talk is complete. A full stomach often equates to a cloudy disposition and lethargy. These are not great ingredients for the consummate communicator we hope to be.

Claim the cliché

Like me, you have been advised by many well-meaning instructors that clichés are unprofessional and should be avoided. Consider this: How does a cliché become a cliché? Aren't these sayings usually factual? The early bird does, in fact, get the worm. However, *early* is a relative term as a later rising winged creature will, likely, imbibe on a later rising worm. In other words, everyone eats; it's just a matter of when and where. *Early* and *late* are relative terms with nebulous results.

With this in mind, use clichés when relevant for impact. Should you practice effective reactive phraseology, you may create clichés of your own which audience members will take with them. Remember, when you seek the diamond in the rough you may end up without a care in the world but always heed the writing on the wall because what goes around comes around. As with all words, use clichés but never allow them to use you. "A stitch in time saves nine." (I still don't get that one.)

Uniqueness

Finally, be aware of your *hook* and maintain it. This is especially important when you serve on a panel of so-called experts. What makes you unique and stand out individually? As you have left behind something following a presentation, also strive to leave a visual reminder.

Very often people forget names but remember the little guy in the mock turtleneck and sports jacket. "Right. That was the guy from McWho Media," or whomever you represent. That's me, the little guy with the big mouth. What's yours? The guy in the red hat? The blue glasses? Cartoon tee and blazer? Important note: Never allow your look to develop into a gimmick; it must flow organically and represent accurately who you are. As in all communication and marketing, image must support the brand. In this instance, you are the brand. Define your image or someone will do it for you!

This brings us roughly to our halfwaypoint.

Armed with the data on the preceding pages, hopefully, you will find a fundamental map to aid in outlining your next mission. Still to come, we go deeper.

Break a lip!

Chapter 7 - Putting It Together

Now that we have discussed methodology, psychology, and terminology, we can begin to build a basis of communicating relevance. Practicing the RELATE, POP, and IT principles discussed in previous chapters provide the launch pad to assembly. In the coming pages, we will discuss foundational issues that cause message erosion and impact destruction.

So, let's go! Often when dealing with sales or talent training, in particular, I find one repetitive issue to cause us to stumble out of the gate. Simply stated, "Before there is an *is*, there was a *was*." Say what? That is to say, nothing happens independently or originally. All stories, sales, and relationships are based in what *was*.

Depending upon your world view, before there was light there was dark. Before there was a one cell organism that evolved, there was the primordial goo from which it sprang. Often knowing the origins of what was will build your case for what is, as well as what should be.

For instance, before cell communication was widespread, and after Morse code, we stayed in touch via beepers. It was a little device that sat on a pocket or in a purse that would provide an irritating sound and printout of a number to be called. At first, only doctors could afford them. As is the case, however, demand shrank the price and everyone had to have one. I realize that to 97.6 percent of you, this has no value. Give me a minute to relate worth.

At the beginning of these consumer marketing plans for pagers/beepers, I was hired by a large paging company to advance this newfangled way of keeping in touch. The task was to communicate the technology on a frontier where consumers were not really even comfortable with ten-digit calling. I have to dial an area code before my number? That's insane! Plus, to make the job even more interesting, the CEO of the paging company was not a fan of anything but print media. As he told me in a meeting, "My marketing team is confident that you can move product. I disagree. I believe one has to see it to get it. Show me."

With that nod of instruction, combined with such a huge vote of confidence, I began my research. I focused first on what was relevant to the man in charge, not on content. To him, it was all about history and the success he found in print. Two things rang out to me in prep, one mentioned; see it to get it, another implied; historically speaking, this is what works. So, with the help of an amazing team, we met him where he lived. We delivered history that he could see with his *ears*.

We began with this premise: How would history have been affected if major role players had pagers/beepers? The copy ideas were endless and the sales material really wrote itself. For example, had Custer worn a beeper, would he have still faced Little Big Horn? If the chief of the Manhattan Indians had a pager, would he still have made the $24 deal with Peter Minuet? You get the idea. We wrote and produced a series of three "Pages out Of History" with a slug line, "Write your own page in history with (client name here)."

The client did not like the idea; he LOVED

it! He was amazed that we did not just try to move his product; we delivered motivational information to consumers that promoted his product, a necessity as opposed to a luxury. Sales boomed and that campaign had legs until the cellular revolution (which was probably three weeks later). I'm kidding, but it was not long, as technology keeps us all challenged and creative.

Herein lies the logic of "Before there is an *is*, there was a *was*." In an effort to advance and grow a consumer base, we must be aware of where the consumers come from to enhance where they are going, while enjoying where they are. As philosopher, writer, and poet, George Santayana said, "Those who cannot remember the past are condemned to repeat it." May I add my footnote: There is no condemnation in repeating the past as long as the desired results are attained. Learn what works and enhance the model.

While the benefits to the marketer seem obvious, the reward of backstory research for the speaker is just as rich. When you take the time to discover the histories of the industry or product you are addressing to those who rely on it, you are making great relational strides. Not only are you speaking with authority, you are showing those in attendance your personal connection to their mission. You are not just another *talking head*; instead, you have become a participant in a shared quest.

Chapter 8 – Brand & Image

How do we become this involved participant with the audience? First, and of great importance, your content has to matter. You genuinely need affection and connection to the data you present. Anything else is an act—not drama. And, drama moves the needle. Acting can elicit apathy from the audience. This goes back to that passion thing we discussed earlier. What matters to your audience must matter to you. If that is true, and you are involved, advance research of the target and their relation to the brand is required. At the root of results, you will usually find a strong brand connection and sense of pride in relationship. This is where we begin to develop personal ownership necessary to present with authority.

If there is one thing I've learned over the years of working inside major media operations, it's the relevance and importance of brand maintenance and protection. As a communicator/marketer, personal knowledge and commitment to the brand and image protection must be without pause. First, however, we must define a "brand." Is it a company, a logo, an institution, or product? Yes.

A brand is the life blood of an organization. It is the reputation built over time that has proven to be sufficient without explanation. During my journey, it has been my extreme pleasure to be associated with brands that are household names— and others of which few outside the hallowed halls of the establishment are familiar. In both cases, a few constants promoted their success.

First, a brand produces an emotional connection immediately upon revelation to an audience. Just hearing the name makes us smile, sigh, frown, or shake our heads. Rarely are our emotions ambivalent if we are familiar with the company, product, or service. We connect to major brands personally because we bring personal experiences to the table as our major source of reference.

For example, in the past, when I would say, "I represent The Walt Disney Company," suddenly there was a tie between myself and the audience based on past experience. Similarly, a level of expectation was heightened based on the audience's past interaction and experience with the company. (Creative excellence, family standards, consumer protection, and credibility come to mind since these are fundamental aspects of the brand of The Walt Disney Company.) That expectancy should, and did, provoke humility on my part since I was saying I have come from the source to share agreed-upon wisdom. Representing yourself is one thing; speaking for a highly respected group should bring a large lump to your throat prior to speaking. For now, you are representing something larger than yourself.

A brand is built over time and nurtured by the hands and deeds of many who have gone before, either those inside the *machine* or those who support the actions. Development is never created in a vacuum. It can be deeply harmed though by individual interactions with a client or consumers who rely upon your expertise and wisdom if you don't represent the brand appropriately. Once you say, "I work for (fill in the blank)," you are not the only one being watched; the credibility of those who have gone before takes center stage as well. The responsibility of brand awareness and protection rests with you. In other words, open the door and you are center stage. **Be the brand and all it represents; its future rests with you.** Dramatic? Yes, but valid. Think about it.

While we agree that it is necessary for you to reflect the brand appropriately, it also falls to you, as the speaker or representative, to be the brand's champion and protector. Unfortunately, negativity, jealousy or, sometimes, deliberate actions can bring tarnish. When this happens, it is up to you to "put on your cape and fly to the brand's aid." You are not responsible for the action of others or are you? In this case, yes, you primarily are. As my father used to say, "If you are going to take the King's shilling, you must fight the King's war." While I'm sure he was not the originator of the line, he was my original source so he gets the credit. When translated, this means that when we agree to represent a brand, we agree to support it in good times and bad.

Ideally, you have joined a team that you respect and can strengthen by your steadfastness to its established integrity. If not, you may need to do some soul searching. Operating from the premise that you *do* believe in whom you serve, brand not individual, be prepared to be a spokesperson of resolve.

What if there are flaws in the brand? What if there is a modicum of truth to the negativity? Then, own it! Bad things happen to good people and companies err when we fail to acknowledge and address the latter. **The unpleasant thing about people representing brands is that people represent brands.** Say, what? Back to the POP principle discussed in Chapter 2. Brand support is affected by perspective, opinion, and personality (POP) in no small way. Therein lies the need for each individual to know the reputation of the brand to effectively support it.

Now that we have established the role we all play in support, we need to determine our responsibility in maintenance. Resting on past successes will often result in future failures leading to erosion of the brand. How does one maintain an inanimate object, such as a brand, that is based deeply on history, reputation, and emotional connections? One remembers the origin and enhances the standards required to keep the brand in good stead.

If your brand is founded on solid

performance and customer service, it becomes everyone's duty to maintain both qualities. For instance, I buy my personal vehicles from a certain auto dealership. My purchase is not based solely on price. While cost is important, customer service is more important in my perspective. In my years of supporting this group, I have *never* had a bad experience post sale. Catch the use of the absolute? "Never" is a big word and the weight is felt by each individual involved in this auto store. It goes beyond convenience—and they are convenient— but client satisfaction seems truly to be *Job #1*.

I have never brought my car in to this dealership for an oil change to be later *up sold*, as few dealers can claim. Instead, I have asked for service that they did not deem necessary and have been talked out of the expense. Say, what? That is brand maintenance. **When you care more about maintaining your brand, your brand will care more about maintaining you.** It is cause and effect.

So, we agree effort is required to support and maintain our brand and that there is an emotional connection to it typically. Now, we go deeper into a much more challenging proposition. How do we keep the brand relevant? There are a myriad of case studies of monolithic companies resting on past successes only to lose market share due to antiquated techniques and beliefs. While no names need mentioning, I point you to the brick and mortar graveyard of businesses that failed to see the relevance of an online presence. Not only have many lost market share, some have become "the showroom" for online merchants.

Beware the gloom and doom naysayers and their go-to phrases:

"That's the way we've always done it."

"We just don't work that way."

"Our way or the highway."

This logic has cost more major brands more than market share. It has cost image destruction beyond repair in many instances.

Perhaps thoughts like these will generate awareness and prosperity:

"We need to rethink our processes."

"Times change. Why haven't we?"

"We've run out of road. Let's follow the detour."

The relevance of a brand depends less on leadership's ability to lead and more on their ability to follow. Often, the very future of the brand is dependent upon this ability.

Longevity and health of a brand is the responsibility of all who touch it and respond to the evolving climate and expectations. However, the fiber that the brand was formed around must be the constant litmus test to properly evaluate directives for the future. For instance, if *family friendly* is the foundation of your brand, then continuous focus and maintenance is mandatory. Once you stray off course you affect our next topic, deeply.

Finally, let's talk "image." While the brand evokes an *emotion*, the image reflecting back on that mother ship provokes a *reaction*. Emotion without reaction is just a feeling, and success based on a feeling is short-lived. Using the car dealer analogy, if you buy on price alone and the service department suffers from mediocrity, wherein lies the value? As is the case in all relationships, business or otherwise, we need to know that the values expressed are reality, not just motives to another destination. In other words, "Don't just tell me you care. Prove it!"

The image portrayed by the individuals representing any brand will affect the consumer's desire to be associated with the brand. Say, what? Reduced to its lowest common denominator, image is the mirror in which our audience sees itself. Does this brand get me? Or, are they trying to get at me? This is one thing often overlooked in communication resulting in resounding failure—talking past your audience as opposed to talking about issues your audience cares about. **Know the room. Know the need. Know the content. Then, speak as one of the audience, not the expert.** You are the future of the brand, the face of the brand, and the hope of longevity. WARNING: You are being watched!

In case you missed it the first time:

> **Brand...evokes an emotion**
> **Image...provokes a reaction**

Print it on a poster; post it on a wall; put it on a t-shirt; emblazon it upon your monogram; or ink it to your person. Regardless, where you place it, protect it. Retain this critical information because you will be tested daily. Your understanding will determine success or failure of the brand far past your involvement.

Chapter 9 – Three W's

If you were paying attention earlier, you remember that this topic first appeared in *the box* that everyone is getting out of. While there are five *W's* found there, no connection to past presidents by the way, we are going to concentrate on the primary three, the first of which is ***who***.

Who?

Knowing the makeup of your audience is more than just important—it is essential. This is not merely cursory knowledge of their names and occupations. While that can be relevant, more important is their place in the circle of influence. Where do they sit in regards to support or non-support of the subject matter, the product or the mission? Will some be wary of your statements or most already be in agreement? In any group setting, you usually find three primary camps.

The first camp is **the core.** These are the ones you should strive to address directly. You will spot them early on in any presentation. Watch the cues, smiles, head nods, and expressions of deep agreement. These are fans that would usually support the concepts all the way to ruin, heaven forbid, but they know what you are saying is true. They believe you. They believe *in* you. Yes, there is a difference.

Remember, there is a big difference between *believe* and *think.* Believers are the bedrock—stronger than any analytical research. There is no need to strive to convince them of relevance. Instead, your challenge is to have them support your methodology and agree on how to implement strategic support. While they may be fans, they will, probably, not follow blindly if your material does not connect with their vision. Tread with care and with awareness; lose the core and your foundation will rapidly crumble.

The majority of your audience will likely fall

into our second category, **the target**. This group could best be categorized as friends. They want to follow and they want to believe but, first, they need to know your motivations, and test your knowledge, and dedication. This is the sweet spot—the ones who will make or break a team. This is not only because they are the majority of attendees, but also because they have the potential to carry more influence. They have come with expectations and, should your message resonate, they will take it to the streets with extreme vigor. A friend turned fan, or core, often brings extreme energy and fresh ideas needed to maintain or revitalize a project or mission. Once they know, they are on the way to believe. Once they believe, the overall core base has increased.

Our third and final group is **the followers**, referred to as "periphery." These are the ones often attending for a free lunch, a day off, or because the boss said so. However, they may also be the most fertile field. These are the thinkers, not in the realm of reasoning or deduction but, the ones deducing there may or may not be value in your information. Nevertheless, everyone likes a free buffet. Someone once said, "If you feed them, they will come," or something similar. Again, they are easy to spot. Once the meal is over and the presentation is in motion, they are the ones checking their watches, leaning on their chins, or playing with their smart phones. (Note: If possible, it is always best to keep your gatherings brief enough to request a smart phone-free zone. Good luck with that.) While the followers are important and deserve notice, this is not the group to build your directives around. At most, you will create some new *friends* from these that will provide a deeper base for your next meeting.

For reference:

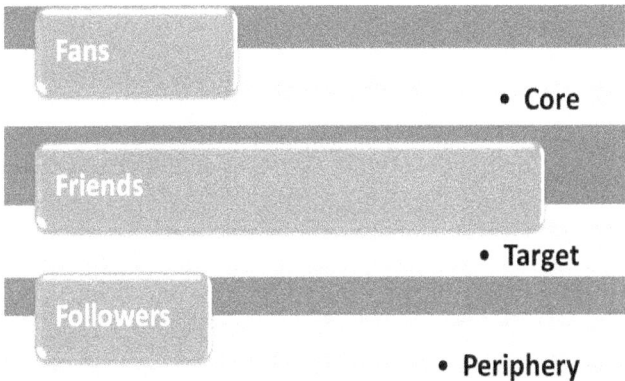

Graphic lines presented are for reference only and are not based on statistical data only from experience. Thorough preparation will address **the target** and its needs for convincing. **The core** should support what is presented and **periphery** should perceive the content as relevant.

Now that we have established the *who* we are hoping to address, let's examine our next W, which is the **what**. This can be a more complicated destination as various factors must be considered aside from subject matter.

What?

First, we must understand the perception surrounding our product, service, or company. Are we need-, want- or impulse-based or a combination of all of the above? Understanding our placement in the landscape of consumer perspective will enable more deliberate and abbreviated discussions. This allows attendees to focus on the mission of communicative marketing.

"Want" or "need"? This is a slippery slope open for negotiation that falls back to the POP principle discussed in Chapter 2. For instance, if you live in a widespread locale such as Dallas or Los Angeles, where your job is often a thirty- to forty-five-minute commute (if you are lucky), a reliable automobile is a *need*. Alternatively, if you reside in a densely populated area, such as New York City, where offices, residences, and public transportation successfully cohabitate, an auto is perhaps a *want*.

For the sake of discussion, let's use the

scenario above regarding a vehicle, with a twist. Our manufacturer is rolling out a new line of vehicles aimed at the "soccer moms"; the line features a sport-utility vehicle (SUV) that functions like a minivan. Our *who*, provided as reference, is an audience of professional people, men and women ranging in age from twenty-five to forty-five years, with a median income of six figures and 2.5 kids. How do we address? What is our *what?* Say, what?

When persuading audiences or moderating focus groups, I have learned the following:

Talk about the CF first—which is the "coolness factor." Even though your audience may live in the suburbs, enjoy sitting poolside, and sipping drinks with umbrellas in them, they are still concerned about the personal perception of their peers. (It's scary how we never seem to get away from that.) Perhaps even more importantly, is the CF perceived by their most important audience— their kids? Almost without exception, parents are remarkably concerned with the *image* they portray to their youngest family members. If your product or idea has that connection, you have crossed a mighty bridge. We go from "Drop me off a few blocks away from school" to "Take me to the front door so my friends can check out this ride and how cool you are."

Once you have established your *coolness,* press on to the practical side of these professional folks. Address factors that are important to them as car owners like efficiency, environment, and ergonomics. How much will all of this innovation cost the planet and your comfort? While the concern for image is important, even those with liquidity want to *save.*

Finally, reinforce the brand of the car (or company, product, service, concept, role, or teaching) and its dedication to preserving its good name with customer service. Let me repeat that, *customer service.* This is where a deal is sealed as opposed to closed because a guarantee of some kind is implied. Realistically speaking, anyone can move a product or have someone buy into an idea, once. Anyone can close a deal. But, a sealed deal is built upon much more than value. It is structured by relationship and the management necessary to maintain it. Repeat business is not always a result of quality but often a result of customer satisfaction with the way one is treated. Say, what?

Don't tell me you appreciate me, show me. **Understand this: Quality is king and the lack thereof is the jester that delivers failure with a laugh.** Quality is expected and deserved. Service is the calling card of repeat relational value. The companies that continue to dominate are those who understand the necessity of customer appreciation and maintenance. This is the heart of the matter that will matter the most.

What about cost? In this environment, cost is irrelevant. You are not here to sell a vehicle; your role is to provide information that will deliver informed consumers to a dealer whose job it is to move a vehicle. Many presentations fail due to a lack of understanding of the *what* they are intended to do. You should present a price range if audience expectations warrant but, you are selling brand and image, not vehicles.

We all want to think our offerings meet a need and consumers should agree and consider it a "must have." The truth is that, before a need is known, it often begins in categories such as "want" or "impulse."

Before I need it, I must want it, and that often begins with an impulse to *try it*. Starting at the base of the pyramid below will often deliver loyal consumers. **Communicative marketing that drives to impulse is the primary mission.**

Follow the logic of the pyramid to establish and maintain market share of whatever you're trying to *sell, be it a product, service, or relationship*.

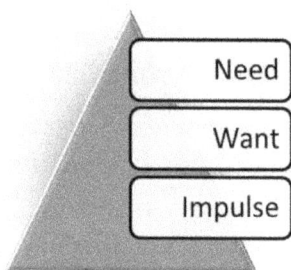

As noted earlier, the most difficult person to sway is the one who thinks in terms of "I don't need it, I already have one." Once a consumer has established a satisfactory relationship with a product, service, or company, they are hesitant to move in another direction. Reasoning for adjustment requires establishing image connection to a brand with equal quality, greater benefits, and customer satisfaction. It's tough. That's where passion on the part of the "communicator" enters the equation with the resolve to serve.

Following the same detailed logic in presenting other known *want* categories will often deliver desired results as the audience is proactively involved on a reactive basis. Adjustment of delivery styles addressed in Chapter 3 may often be required, as demographics will vary. While, the journalistic style may speak to the baby boomer, the millennial may be more responsive to your lifestyle approach. Focus groups and studies I have been involved with through the years find that males, ages 25-44, are quick enactors of technology/entertainment products. Females in same demographic, however, are more predictably responsive to cosmetic treatments as in home improvements, personal grooming, and family merchandise. I'm not sure what that says about the two genders, but there must be a story there.

Regardless of target, attention must be paid to credibility and substantiation during your delivery. Remember, absolutes such as *best* and *greatest* are irrelevant since we have been bombarded with those allegations before. Allow your dialogue to focus on fact-based findings and research that impacts lives and the absolutes will write themselves.

This relates nicely to our final W, **why**.

Why?

Why should anyone trust you or even care about the data you espouse? If you are representing a brand that is backed by an image of respectability, therein lies the answer. As was told to me on several occasions by my dear departed, gray-haired mother, "You are known by the company you keep."

In my travels with major television and radio networks, I was usually greeted with honor and warm regard because of the ones who had gone before me and their attention to credibility retention. It was much easier to gain access to people when representing a major brand as opposed to just being me. This is called "standing on the shoulders of greatness." **Before you take on the name of the brand, be aware of those who took it on before you.** Their reputation is on the line with every word you speak and action you take. While he has been gone a while, Walt Disney's good name remains intact due, in no small part, to leadership that understood his legacy and strives to continue his call.

Of equal importance is to remember that one slip can have devastating results on the *why* we support a brand. Too many times, great companies and people have fallen due to an error in judgment or quick reactions. Back to the military analogies of my father, "Define the hills you will die on" and from my mother, "Your actions represent a family (brand) not just your own, so mind your tongue."

Hills worth giving your life for are few, and protecting the reputation of others matters more than your own. It can take years to build the house and only one bolt of lightning to bring it down.

With that, we wrap up our *W's*. I know there are two others, **when** and **where**. Those are fundamental in communication for event planning but rarely of concern in presentations. Of relevance and worth mentioning is, **when** you present, you should be aware of timing. That is to say, know when to speak and when not to speak. In regards to **where**, strive to keep the content universal with personal opinions minimized. One final W you might use upon completion of your presentation preparation—whew!

I trust that, by now, you are beginning to realize the efforts required to thoroughly address a topic with relevance and impact. Communication is work. Great communication is hard work! Truth!

Chapter 10 – Mind Your
P's and Q's

Many years ago, I was contracted by a major restaurant chain to develop a marketing campaign to attract family business. I still remember the initial conversation with the founder of the operation. He told me the canvas was blank and that he was hopeful I had the brushes and colors needed to bring his vision to life. For years, evening business had thrived and the bar was constantly full, but the weekend lunch crowd was nonexistent, and he felt he was missing a major opportunity. I sat and politely nodded, taking notes, and asking fundamental questions regarding menu, staffing, costs, and decor primarily. We established a timeline, shook hands, and agreed to meet in two weeks.

The next day was Saturday, so I made a trip in for lunch, incognito. I have always held to the logic that sampling a product or service as a consumer without fanfare is the most accurate way of revealing strengths and weaknesses. The owner was right; this was one dead grill. The folks were friendly, the food fantastic, and the atmosphere amenable. But nothing said "family," nothing that hit our first of three *P's* of success, **personal**. On the flip side of that, the bar area was hopping. Even at 11:30 am, it was loud, rowdy, and rocking. This is fine if that is your deal, but if you are a family of five, not so much.

Before we can connect to our audience on any valuable level, our content, product, or mission must contain an element of personal connection that relates to the core. In this case, his core—bar goers—had the connection, but his target, families, was not happening. My first note: How important is family business to his business model?

This takes us to our second P, **powerful.** In an effort to cause a target to overflow into a periphery, our messaging must possess power. To the point that our audience can not only connect with our content, but also takes pride in being associated with it, in this example, we had a bit of a divided camp. We had patrons very comfortable with the cold adult beverages, loud volume, and boisterous companions giving a sense of power in numbers and association. Conversely, we had an owner charged with increasing his family business and feeling powerless to do so. The use of power in this sense is not one of control, but one of camaraderie and connection. Here's the dilemma: Can power be restored to both camps? Yes, it can, but not without cost and consideration.

Bringing us to our final P, **pliability**, before we can address where we want to go, we need to address our satisfaction level with where we are. Say, what? Be it good or bad, there are those who are totally satisfied with where they stand and have no desire to pursue market share increases aggressively. This is the *reactive* team whose philosophy is: "If it ain't broke, don't fix it."

Then there are those who always think change is needed to grow. "If it ain't broke, break it; build it stronger with the pieces." This would be the *proactive* team. Both require pliability to maintain or grow their business. The only constant is change while only change is constant.

In which camp does our owner land? As is the case most often, both camps. He is making budget and filling a need for his core. However, he is losing possible gains by not actively pursuing a rapidly growing target.

Following research, my proposal was going to involve cost initially to validate both teams in providing personal connection and powerful ownership. Option 2 would be to focus on serving a single audience with occasional periphery participation—in this case, the bar patrons who also may have lunch or dinner.

What did the owner do? He followed the observations from current and possible future patrons and decided to focus on what was and gradually grow what could be. Monday through Friday was business as usual. On weekends, the bar did not open until 4 pm and family fare and entertainment like interactive table games and karaoke were a part of the weekend mid-day activities.

He took success as a **personal** goal, allowed his patrons to have **power,** and was **pliable** enough to go against the original model.

He chose a hill and continued up it!

Minding your P's and Q's will improve audience relations and deliver success far past expectations.

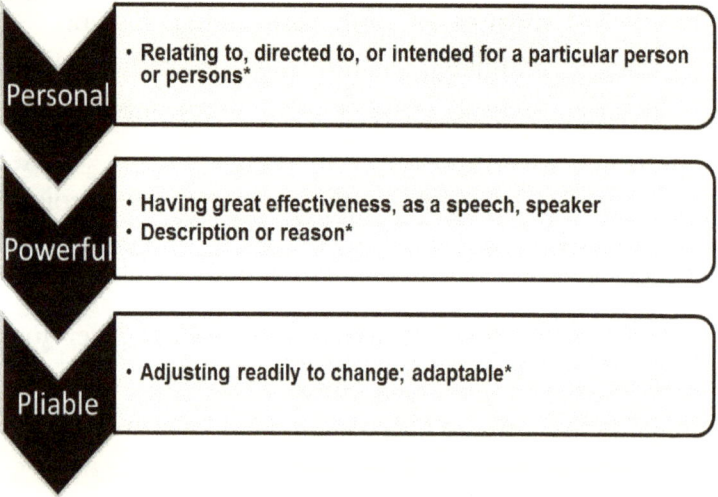

Personal
- Relating to, directed to, or intended for a particular person or persons*

Powerful
- Having great effectiveness, as a speech, speaker
- Description or reason*

Pliable
- Adjusting readily to change; adaptable*

*Dictionary.com Unabridged. Based on the Random House Dictionary,
© Random House, Inc. 2015.

In regards to our Q's:

Be prepared to ask **questions** beyond the superficial. Oftentimes you will be surprised how amenable a client is to the tough queries.

- Do you really want to succeed?
- Are you prepared to do what it takes?
- If the research goes against plan are you willing to take a risk?

- How deep are your pockets?

Q2, practice **quiet** time. In other words, listen closely to responses and observe the passion that's behind them.

Finally, in our Q land…remember that success is a **quest** not often immediately gratified. Make sure your client is aware that time, patience, and yes, money will be required to realize the dream.

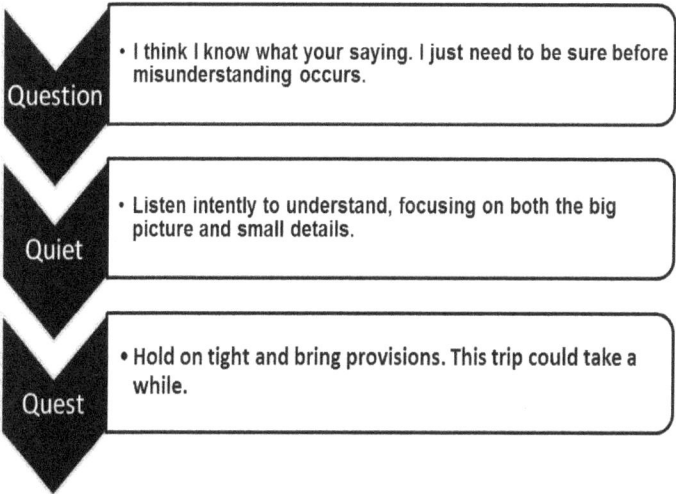

Question	• I think I know what your saying. I just need to be sure before misunderstanding occurs.
Quiet	• Listen intently to understand, focusing on both the big picture and small details.
Quest	• Hold on tight and bring provisions. This trip could take a while.

Chapter 11 – Three R's

I grew up in the Dark Ages, slightly after the earth cooled, and the dinosaurs were no more. This was back in the days when education was focused on fundamentals and the three R's as they were called: reading, 'riting and 'rithmetic. Dropping the first letter of the latter two allowed for the alliteration which remains burned into my mind to this day. Please do not surmise that I think today's education model is flawed. Education, like all life, must evolve to meet the demands of each generation. I use the Dark Ages to allow for foundational development of styles. That alone is the reference. Whew! I hopefully dodged those emails from friends and colleagues currently shaping the minds of tomorrow.

Effective communicators should also embrace a non-exclusive set of three R's to allow for greater development, creatively and informationally. Prior to venturing down this road, please know that it will go against the grain and seem illogical. But, if you allow yourself to think back to a time when you had an open mind, it just might make sense. Thus, and therefore, we begin.

First of all, prior to launch of preparation, **relax.** This is a very simple word with amazing power to the presenter, marketer, or speaker. Before I begin any prep work, I find my happy place—my sanctuary, my focus factory. As stated earlier, for me it is a neighborhood walk that allows me to empty my mind of concerns and focus on the fundamentals I need to address my topic. Note: To relax does not mean to disconnect from the mission. Rather, it means to remove an environmental distraction that reduces focus. This is when you "outline" your known needs and ponder the possible unknowns. In this place, you can begin to clearly define objectives—both yours and the client's.

Personal objectives often remain constant:

- To be clear and understood
- To be factual and informative
- To be relational
- To be invited back

The client's objectives, on the other hand, will vary greatly due to product/brand differences as well as anticipated demographic/gender differences of attendees. The geographical location of meetings will also have an effect. Be aware of the differences in acceptable styles dependent upon locale. You smile, but a presentation delivered on the West Coast will come across much differently in the Midwest. Trust me. **Know who you are talking too *but also* where you are.**

Some constants remain:

- Brand
- Image
- Target (core and periphery)
- Market share
- Attributes
  - Positive
  - Negative
- Public acceptance
- Staff morale

Before you put pen to paper, fingers to keys, or voice to record, allow these considerations to run free in your mind. Doing so will provide the supplies you need to paint the overall picture you desire.

Once you have established the information you perceived with broad strokes, the second R, **research,** comes into play. This is the area where what is *thought* meets what is *known* to advance to what should be. Say, what? This is where the work begins!

In your relax mode, you were, hopefully, able to focus on a self-made scenario, analytically viewing the status of primary points from the outside. This is perceptive research, based heavily upon personal viewpoints and conversations with others not associated with the product/service. Now, you take that data and begin formulating a base for the presentation. You spend advance time with senior management to capture the vision, concern, and plans. Then take a moment with the mid-level team, the workers on the floor, to uncover similarities and differences in motivation and observation. Finally, the support staff, administrative assistants, manager trainees, clerical personnel, and the people holding the important role of receptionist. (Sarcasm is neither intended nor implied.)

   The receptionist is the primary point person or initial face of any company. This person is the first one the public sees, hears, and interacts with in person. In my opinion, you hire a team. You cast a receptionist. Enough preaching for now, just know this is a major job.

   Fundamental knowledge required from all includes:

- Time with company
- Brand perception
- Image contributions
- Mission
- Target audience
- Morale
  - Personal
  - Perceived
- Public relations

   While not an exhaustive list, this will provide basic data needed to help you connect with your audience. This information will not be your content but it should drive your motivation and influence the development of talking points. For example, profits are down, image is uncertain, leadership is not trusted, and morale is horrendous.

With this information, you can begin to develop a story to address overall direction and agreed upon mission.

From the inside environment, you go to the exterior to find known concerns or praises from consumers or vendors. This information is usually easily obtained from Internet sources and consultations with known participants.

Fundamental information sought includes:

- History of company
- Reputation
- Service records
- Reviews
- Competition overview

Once you're satisfied that you have the needed fundamental information, your presentation preparation can begin.

The cosmetic assembly will depend upon your personal preferences and the technology available. But fundamentally, most effective communication can reference the model below.

- **Remember where you were** (Before there is an *is*, there was a *was.)*

- **Know where you're going** (Without a destination, travel is exhausting at best.)

- **Enjoy the** journey (Be aware of waypoints and the wisdom offered.)

- **Never be afraid to ask for directions** (You're not the first to travel this road. Learn from fellow sojourners.)

Our final R is **rehearse**. Outside of the arts/media industry, I find this is often the most challenging activity for communicators. After all, they say, "I have my data, my presentation: my slides are clear and my story complete." All may be true, but until you hear it, you don't know its credibility. **What may read well and feel full may ring empty when presented with the wrong inflection, direction, or diction.**

A pro knows how to dramatize and glamorize otherwise mind-numbing data into relatable material with punch. It's not what we say, but how we say it that leaves a mark so, rehearse,

rehearse, and rehearse. You just might not believe what you hear coming out of your mouth.

Again, it's not about the acting, it is all about the drama that drives results.

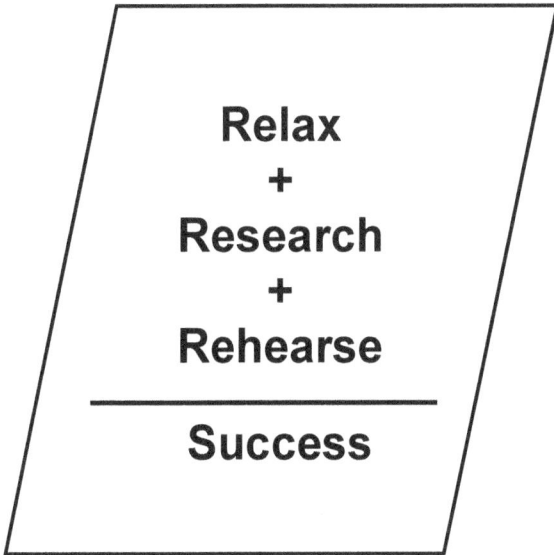

$$\frac{\text{Relax} + \text{Research} + \text{Rehearse}}{\text{Success}}$$

Chapter 12 – Get Your Act Together

While presenting information, selling a product, demonstrating benefits, or speaking before a large group is not, in itself, acting, it's helpful to embrace the elements of the craft that exist. Understanding fundamentals of the art will not only assist in keeping the audience interested, but will develop greater confidence in you as the presenter.

This book is in no way, nor is it meant to be, an acting course. Years of study and guidance in the craft are required to achieve success in *that* arena. Instead, I am presenting a fundamental overview of styles and methods to aid in a limited scope with your mission—more of an enhancement to realize the tools you already possess will help you in delivering confidently. If your destination is the stage or screen, please seek professional training.

In life as in business, while you are not an actor, you are required to act. Say, what? As discussed earlier, we are all called upon daily to deliver material personally and professionally that requires flair and embellishment. To that end, we go to the well of personal interaction and draw upon experience.

Who has influenced you along the way? If you had to address their style, how would you name it? What techniques best speak to you? Perhaps the most challenging questions of all are the ones we rarely ponder. Who are you demographically, intellectually, and personally? Is that perception based on reality or on facts shared by those you trust? Your personality will weigh heavily on your style, and you need to be aware of both internal and external opinions.

Oddly enough, your thoughts about yourself, as they relate to effectively reaching an audience, are irrelevant. While self-adulation often borders on narcissism, it can be illuminating but is rarely beneficial to your presentation. That is to say, what you think of yourself as a communicator doesn't matter, really. However, the thoughts of others bring truth to the adage, "Perception is reality." What people say about us is often the result of who we are as portrayed by our actions. You've heard it before, "Actions speak louder than words." That is truth!

Remember earlier when I mentioned having an open mind? It is very important to have one now. Here we begin working on character development based on your accumulated parts. When leading groups of speakers, teachers, dramatists, or just regular people longing to improve communication skills, this is where I see the greatest revelations combined with the greatest hesitation to participate by attendees. This is the eulogize exercise! Please do not think me morbid with the next analogy; it is a reality that shapes who we are.

One day, in the very, very distant future you and I will be a memory. Okay, that is a nice way of saying one day we will pass away, expire, go home...die. There, I said it. I know this is odd. But hang with me; there are benefits to pondering the inevitable and the happenings thereafter.

Depending upon your requests and preferences, there will probably be some type of gathering to commemorate you and all that you did. And, if I might add, all you did *not* do. Those thoughts will be shared in whispered tones as if you were still around to debate their validity. Said meeting will also include a gathering of friends and colleagues to reminisce and reflect publicly. Some call this a funeral; others call it a memorial, and a few even call it a party, complete with a buffet following in hopes to draw attendees.

Having been an experienced attendee to all of the above, I note no more awkward moment than the "open microphone" portion of the service. This is where the leader says, "I am sure (name) meant a lot to many of you. Now, I would like to open the floor for comments." Then you sit, looking around the room, and making mental notes of the nervousness. Awkward becomes painful when a long silence ensues. Is it that no one has good things to say? Finally, mercifully, even someone does step to the front to speak. A collective sigh of relief is practically heard.

"I remember (name) as a great person of business."

Business!? Sounds like a quote from Charles Dickens' *A Christmas Carol*.

"He/she taught me do be aware of the deal and strive for success."

Yep, there stands Ebenezer Scrooge waxing philosophically on Marley. Please.

This is where awkwardness turns to solemnity. Sure, it's great that they promoted success and mentored you along that path, but what else? There must have been more to the lesson. Did they model integrity, honesty, family focus, and camaraderie? While they taught how to be successful, was it to their advantage or to yours? So, what does this have to do with you and your ability to communicate? Everything. Perception may not be reality but, to the perceiver, it is truth. Say, what? Where a person *has been* is our reference point of what that person is or in this case, was.

Sorry, I know we got a little dark. But, your credibility as a human plays no small role in your ability to communicate and your impact.

Enough backstory, let's begin…The Eulogize Exercise!

First, you are sitting among the attendees at your funeral and the microphone is open. Who speaks and what do they say? Do you agree with the speaker's comments or are they based on presumptions as opposed to reality? Next, you are given the opportunity to offer your own eulogy or possibly rebut the ones prior. What is your content? I ask the same question. Are you being honest or hopeful?

This exercise is not intended to make soul searchers out of anyone. Rather, it is offered to allow us to better understand our portrayal and what audience perception is based upon. You see, while we are the sum of our collective parts, we can subtract or add to that total in a way to benefit our *bottom line* in relational value. That should be your ultimate goal.

This is also not intended to change who you are or how you present yourself. To the contrary, the intent is to identify your strengths in relating. Say, what? You get it. Before the thoughts escape, finalize your efforts by committing your eulogy to the page. Write it down, read it aloud, and then hide it away! This is a personal document intended for an audience of one. From time to time, you will probably edit the content as you become more aware of needed adjustments.

What I have just described, in the acting world, is known as character development. In this case, though, it is the character that is developing you which allows you to develop others. Please do not overlook or laugh off this type of training. **When we have the nerve to investigate what drives us, we are poised to drive others.** It's also nice to know friends and family will attend your goodbye party to celebrate your life as opposed to the buffet that should follow.

While, again, this is not an acting course, it is relevant to mention a basic knowledge of method versus character acting skills to enhance presentations.

Reduced to their lowest common denominators:

- **Method acting depends on the action of others to promote reaction.** When time and content allows, this can be a very effective style. However, caution is advised as open involvement can lead to over elaborative messaging followed by lack of direction and minimal retention. As the leader, it is imperative in this environment that you allow for relevant exchanges without editorial reflection

- **Character acting is the art of working alone, finding reaction to content as opposed to others.** This is where the power of interpretation, knowledge of demographics, and aptitude of attendees, mission awareness, and shared interests provide the backdrop. Reacting to

known realities in those areas will
develop the event character and allow
for the creative freedom required by you
to effectively communicate

Independent of the acting style used, one
constant remains: You are driving the data, and you
must retain ownership via confidence from start to
finish. Relinquishing authoritative control to
participants, by allowing their drawn out narratives
straying often from point will erode messaging
resulting in diminishing return on investment and
loss of credibility. All voices are welcome as long as
their messages are pertinent.

Chapter 13 – Some Assembly Required

As we head down to the finish line of effectively communicating professionally and personally, it is important to assemble our outline, content, and format. Follow the simple three-step procedure of 1) setup 2) elaboration and 3) culmination and your design should permit natural progression toward closure.

"Setup" could also be called the stretching exercise that allows you and your audience to prepare for the detailed information to follow. Building on brand awareness and image support is the mainstay of this step. Depending upon your final destination, special attention should be paid to agreed standards and substantiated data related to company expectations. As in any creative endeavor, this is a critical portion of your meeting. It should be designed to *hook* interest with known qualities while providing a launch into less familiar assumptions. Following is an example.

*Welcome to the fundamentals of XYZ Inc., a brand **we all know** and, hopefully, are **proud to represent**—a company built around more than just leadership expectations but also grown, thanks **to the trust** of our consumers.*

"I have yet to have a bad experience with XYZ. Their quality meets expectations; their service surpasses."

"Johnny, my rep with XYZ, has always kept me informed as to the status of my account."

"XYZ has my business, period!"

*As a member of the XYZ team, you should **take pride in the impact you** are making and the results your efforts are bringing forth. According to recent market studies, our satisfaction ratings are higher than ever before and sales are following suit. This is due, in no small part, to the **roles you are playing** in regards to our image support and customer service—the things that are the backbone of our history and the promise of future success. For that, be proud!*

Words in bold provide ownership to the audience while maintaining objectivity by implication. While everyone may not agree with these assertions, no one can argue with the client observations, in quotations. This provides the data to back up the stated stance of "take pride" in what you do. Noteworthy is the verbiage, "proud to represent," as opposed to "where you work." Employment is often considered a means to an end. It is the way we support our family, feed ourselves, and avoid walking around naked. It is important, but of very limited relevance to the *pride* referenced.

The word "represent," however, implies ownership, at least mental ownership, which often yields a more attentive audience since you seem personally involved. The next step of promoting pride in the impacts being made personally, not corporately, further adds to the need for individuals and the talents they deliver. Finally, emphasis on roles being played allows for a greater connection as contributors are appreciated for individual contributions. The final implication is that all in attendance are the backbone of XYZ and, as such, play a tremendous role in the company's future.

While setup is the *stretch* of our exercise, elaboration would be the spirit or the heart of the workout. This is where ownership of results are individually maintained while recognizable areas of improvement are shared. Say, what?

> While **we all** have much to be grateful for and excited about, we must also be mindful of opportunities **to adjust,** as necessary and as the business climate shifts.
>
> As noted earlier, we have always been aware of our status in regards to brick and mortar, but that environment is shifting. **Are we shifting** with it?
>
> Note the numbers... (comparative data with primary competitors)
>
> **If,** as **individuals,** we take ownership of the realities in the ever-evolving nature of business and utilize the strengths **we** possess, as team members, we are confident that the brand we have built will not only stand the test, but exceed expectations. This is because those **expectations** are founded on the desire of **each of you** in this room.

The elaboration stage is where we put the message of *team* out there, not to stroke egos, but because it is reality—paying close attention to the use of "we" as the case is built for collaborative efforts. While many are involved in success and, of course, most want to own it, there are a select few willing to admit to the need for *change* in their own direction if industry is to keep evolving. Beware of using the word "change," as it implies that something is broken. A better choice of terms is "adjustments" because most people can agree that periodic adjustments are needed.

Once a team is established, returning to

individual efforts delivers greater support and, likely, agreement. Note a very special word, *if*. This is a very small word but, perhaps, the most powerful one when used in an elaboration and culmination. It assigns ownership for accountability and, thus, provides a launch for expectations across all involved. When attendees are allowed to participate in both the fulfilling of corporate plans and initial planning, we have lift off!

Finally, let's talk about culmination as in the beginning, not the end. Say, what? When we wrap up a meeting, demonstration, sales call, or conversation there must be that circling back to initial logic for implementation.

> We can agree that XYZ's continued market dominance is a **team effort** and that success, in no small way, is dependent upon each **person in this room**. We've seen the research and heard from consumers. Now what are we prepared to do?
>
> I have heard you say...
>
> Now, it is your move. Take this data to your workspace, **brainstorm with one another** and commit to the success we all not only seek, but deserve. No matter where your place is on the org chart, **you are vital** to our growth, image, and the continuation of this **great brand.**

Here we are, back where we started. The

difference is that now we are successfully marrying the concept of individuality and team efforts. While holding each other and ourselves accountable going forward, we share the outcome. Note the need to tie individual efforts, regardless of status on a ledger, to success. As stated before, there is no unimportant role in the success of a mission, a company, or relationship. Those who thrive understand the complexity of that simple truth. If you have trouble with this logic, try being your own assistant for a day, serve as receptionist, and make a direct call. With perspective of the support team, you will realize the value of all.

By the way, the content above is an example of flow only. Your material will vary based on your company objectives and expected results. I know you knew that but I was advised to say it, just in case. Sheesh, lawyers! I love them.

Chapter 14 – Acting Up

While this is not an acting course, as stated repeatedly, understanding some fundamentals of the craft should prove beneficial. I present the following information not with the intention to adjust who you are, but to help you understand others better. You see, acting or delivering is reacting to what has happened in relation to anticipating what will occur next. Say, what?

While you address an audience in need of your service, or a colleague in need of direction, or a child seeking understanding of a decision, recognizing their motivations and backstories will serve as a great guide to what you should share.

Again, this is not about changing who you are; it is about a greater realization of who your audience is.

With this in mind, I offer two exercises best conducted in group settings and corporate retreats. But, effectiveness can also be realized when approached seriously away from a group setting, provided you are willing to recruit others to analyze and provide constructive criticism on your efforts. This is where your comfort levels will be tested and getting back in the box will be your first thought. Fight it! When you are able to embrace another person's reality and personality, you are on your way to achieving relational and professional bliss. Trust me on this.

Up first, monologues. Coming from the root word, "mono," meaning *one,* combined with "log," meaning *hard,* this exercise is not for the weak. By *monologue-ing,* we are able to get outside of ourselves to see through others' eyes.

Points to ponder prior to delivery are:
- Read the content as information
- Read as entertainment
- Read interpretively, allowing words the power they possess
- Develop a back-story of character portraying

- Understand their origins and the effect on content
- Deliver in *all* styles noted in Chapter 3
  - Straight Ahead
  - Journalistic
  - Lifestyle
  - Humor

Note that I did not say pick one style. Instead, provide personality to each style to enhance validity for a wider audience.

When you begin preparing your delivery using the different styles, it is important that you are "off script." In other words, you are presenting from memory. This promotes development of passion and greater understanding of the content and ability to empathize. Easy, right? Great. Because, once you have mastered the intended delivery and relational goals, the second exercise is to write, direct, and deliver original content. It just keeps getting easier.

Following our mastery of monologues we enter into a serious, personality-stretching exercise, improvisation, or as I like to call it, "working without a net."

Improvisation is when scenario enhancement meets personality development—a blank canvas allows for total design of story, direction, character development, and motivation. This should be easy for everyone since we all do it every day. We are constantly being called upon to address situations with limited data but expectations of clarity. For instance, examples of my responses during childhood and school days include:

- We had homework?!
- My dog ate it!
- The sun was in my eyes!
- Oh, you meant not to eat that last piece, really!

You get the idea. The initial responses are noted above; the improvisation follows.

"We had homework?! That is news to me and I apologize. If you remember, I was not feeling well at all on Friday, and I left school early. Perhaps, you made that assignment after I left."

To which the response was:

"No, it was on the board in clear sight for all to write down as it is every day."

A sad expression was required along with a head shake.

"I apologize for my lack of attentiveness. I was so feverish; I failed to write it down because all I could think about was getting home to bed. May I make it up and bring it tomorrow?

A smile creeps upon the teacher's face.

"That will be fine. Thank you for being so responsible."

Some or all of the above can be based on truth and the outcome was not one of disregard. The offer to complete the assignment was genuine and welcomed. That is necessary improvisation resulting in closure, satisfaction, and an enjoyable three-day weekend.

You may be asking yourself why these exercises are necessary. Following are four reasons:

- **They improve cognitive function**
- **They exercise the mind**
- **They promote mental well-being**
- **They allow for creative release**

But, the universal reality I offer to those on retreats and corporate gatherings is:

It's fun!

From eight to 80, if we are honest, we enjoy being someone else every now and then. For that moment, we are able to forget the things that tie us down and hold us back. We are allowed to live through another scenario, often foreign to us, which grows us relationally and professionally. These role plays are designed to help you understand the different personalities you will encounter on your journey.

In the coming pages, you will find sample scripts for monologues along with character outlines and descriptive scene information for improvisation. For many, this will be the most challenging exercise you have ever attempted, and I have had some refuse to participate. I would encourage you to play along and allow yourself to climb out of that box everyone seems to keep in the center of the room. **When we shift perspective and force ourselves into uncomfortable environments, we typically gain insight that allows greater communication and human interaction.**

Chapter 15 – Action!

Before we delve into the monologue scripts, may I offer a few considerations that could enhance the experience and deliver greater results? Once you have chosen your monologue, read it factually at least twice. After digesting the content and allowing yourself to ponder the story, then the work of relating begins.

In character development, as discussed earlier, nothing just happens; something always occurred prior. People and events are the result of many layers of life. Take the time to flesh out and create a backstory for the person you will portray and their locale. We all came from somewhere and, while we were there, we developed baggage that we continue to carry. This requires a little creative thinking which, for many, can be a challenge. However, allowing this thought process to develop and yourself to design the person produces insight and drama that should make your performance more memorable to the audience.

As you prepare, think about these aspects of your character:

- Who are you portraying?
- What is your age/gender?
- Where do you come from?
- Do you come from a large family?
- Are you an only child or do you have several siblings?
- What is your education level?
- What is your occupation?
- Are your parents living? If so, what are they like?
- What other things are unique to your story line?

Consideration of the above will allow you to determine attention necessary in each style of delivery.

As a reminder, they are:

- Straight ahead – Say it!
- Journalistic – Report it!
- Lifestyle – Live it!
- Humor – Laugh about it!

Be aware of non-verbal actions required for the character you've created. Different backgrounds will develop distinct personalities and body language expressions. Remember, while words are the backdrop, actions are the scenery; allow each to enhance the messaging.

Let me share a quick story. Many years ago, my team was tasked with creating content for an up-and-coming egg producer. The client request was "Capture the feel of the farm and the freshness of the product. We are not just another chicken coop!" So, the brainstorming began. We tossed out ideas about a pretty day accompanied by soft music and pastoral surroundings. How glorious it would be to wake every day to that! As the ideas began to breed upon that consideration, I noted one writer in the back of the room scribbling furiously and chuckling softly. Eventually, all heard his self-absorption and brainstorming ceased while we all looked his way expectantly. He caught our gaze in his peripheral vision and stopped writing.

Cautiously, he said.

"So, this farm setting is nice and relatable but...."

Therein lies the birth of a backstory...*but,*—with that word, interest shifts and avenues open.

"...but?" I said.

He proceeded softly.

"It's predictable. Don't you think?"

Watching heads nodding in agreement, he continued.

"What if we take it from the hen's perspective—what it's like being a part of the greatest team in the national chicken league?"

"Wow!" was collectively heard around the table.

"Not everyone makes the team! Only the top producers with the best quality!"

From that brief interchange and open dialogue, Helen the hen and Rodney the rooster were born. The leader of the National Chicken League (NCL) headquartered at the client's ranch.

"(Client Name), The National Chicken League, not just another chicken coop!"

We loved it. The client? Not so much. Helen and Rodney, you might say, died in development. Was this a failure? Far from it. While that campaign never made it to the air, the team worked and developed content outside the realm of reality. This yielded greater collaboration for future campaigns that used the same logic with great results.

The lesson reinforced: There are no bad ideas in brainstorming. The client, by the way, went with the first idea of soft music and sunrises. They sold some eggs and seemed happy with the results but I still wonder, if allowed to take it down the other road, if a brand and image could have been developed to generate a deeper customer loyalty base. Perhaps we'll never know. I do know that the exercise was beneficial to me creatively and strategically, benefiting many clients since.

I share this to say when you develop your backstory and methodology, it may not connect with everyone. However, dramatic interaction is often more productive to the individual presenting. If content does not speak to you, then you will probably not dedicate the needed resources mentally to convey the content to others.

Next, deliver deliberately, non-apologetically, and with the passion the methodology requires. To be effective as communicators we must *own* our material; never let it own us. Say, what? Everything is up for interpretation depending upon the receiver. But, you, as the presenter, have the backstory to support your strategy. Stay the course!

So, let's do this.

Chapter 16 – Monologues

Now that you are familiar with the basics of monologues and their usefulness in content delivery, the next few pages offer sample scripts. Spend some time with the material and determine the primary style suited to the topic and your personality as an exercise in character development.

Monologue 1 – "Good Morning, I Think"

"The sun rose today. I am uniquely aware because I am a participant in the warmth that followed. I am under the impression that it was a gradual arrival but I, honestly, could not testify to that truth. For you see, it was up full prior to my entrance. The last thing I remember, it was dark and the next time I opened my eyes, it was not. I suppose the illumination first sensed could have been that of the ambient room lighting. But, upon further investigation, it was the sun that streamed through my window beckoning a beginning or, for some, perhaps the end. Regardless, I am in the midst of a sunny day and all the excitement it contains. Wait; are those clouds on the horizon moving in my direction? Oh, they are...what will this do to the glow? Will night overcome the light prematurely? Will the day that started so brightly fade in sharpness and clarity? What about the sun? Wait, it's still there just taking a momentary break in the action to recharge perhaps. Occasionally, the curtains close around it to be followed by an encore presentation as it peeks out from behind the gray. I get it...darkness is momentary and must always give way to the light. Maybe there is something to learn there. But first, breakfast...."

Monologue 2 – "Thanks, Uncle Bill"

"We buried Uncle Bill today. Well, we didn't. We witnessed the farewell and attended the event. The actual burial was something paid for and better handled by the professionals. The details aside, it was an interesting day. Sitting in the hall prior to the procession to the cemetery, I was taken by the silence. It seemed, for one brief moment, my own life was on hold, and I was allowed not to say goodbye to my favorite uncle, but to celebrate his life. It was weird; he was there but he wasn't. I was there but could not attest to what was around me. Strange, but cool. I thought about the times we spent together fishing and sharing hopes. He was the smartest guy I ever knew. Not *book* smart, but *smart* smart—like knowing that happiness is a decision, not a destination. Love is not a feeling, but a commitment. And hard work is not a labor, but a lifestyle. He was pretty sharp for an old guy with a tenth grade education. You see, the war came and he just had to serve. He also taught me that you fight for what matters and for those unable to fight. Yeah, they buried Uncle Bill today. Me? I just said, 'See ya later!'"

Monologue 3 – "I'll Have Pie!"

"I waddled up to the counter and took myself a seat.

Waiting for the waiter as I pondered what to eat.

Was it steak or chicken or perhaps vegan I will try?

But a glance across the counter was the clincher, I'll have pie!

There was cherry, apple, peach, and something they called mincemeat.

Not sure what that one is, but not something I care to eat.

Wait, there's cobbler and there's cake and bowls of pudding, too.

Are those donuts, cupcakes, and cinnamon rolls dripping in sugary goo?

The waiter was approaching, a decision I must make,

I started wanting pie, but now consider chocolate cake.

You know a cruller with coffee could be an option, I think.

For the sophisticates are often seen with a donut and a drink.

My eyes caught the words, 'Today's special: Pecan Pie and Ice Cream.'

If this is not reality, please do not wake me from the dream.

The waiter stood before me, 'Have you made a decision, my friend?'

I sighed, 'Yes, I'll have the salad.' For my spouse had just walked in."

Monologue 4 – "Growing Up"

"What do I want to be when I grow up? It seems a funny question to pose at any age.

The pressure of the right answer weighs on the shoulders of all who dare to ponder.

Regardless of your station in life, 'growing up' seems a relative term. Do you mean grow up as it relates to the calendar? Or, is the reference to taking responsibilities associated with making adult decisions? I can vote at 18 and drink at 21. Are those the benchmarks in question to the observations requested? What do I want to be, then?

Also, do you mean vocationally, personally, or something else in regards to growing up?

I could be an engineer, a doctor, or lawyer professionally, and yet not grow up in the eyes of some. Or, I could be 16 and tops in my class, delivering speeches on the level of those way past my peers, yet still with no means of support.

Am I grown up? You see, this question of growing up is not singular. It is dependent on many factors—some out of the individual's control. Role models, environment, family history, and relationships all contribute to the final result. So, if you have to know, like right now, what I want to be when I grow up, I must answer, 'I choose not to grow up.'

Time will make that decision. Thanks for asking, and pass the mustard, please."

Monologue 5 – "Lost?"

"I would like to clear up a misconception as it relates to the location I find myself in.

Regardless of my final destination, my current locale is on the way and, therefore, cannot be misconstrued as off course, misdirected, nor am I in any way lost. There are those, in this room, who believe I should have stopped a few miles back and asked for assistance or, as they said, 'directions.' These would be needless delays since my vehicle is equipped with GPS—as is my phone, my tablet, and laptop. I have entered data into all four and, okay, perhaps they are providing different means to the same end, leaving me to choose which one to follow. I choose none of the above because I have made this journey on several occasions, and I firmly disagree with the directives being offered. Therefore, I choose to go by memory, allowing for sightseeing along the way.

Had I not, for instance, taken the off-ramp under construction, I would not have been living the adventure we are now involved in. Oh sure, we would be home by now, but devoid of the memories I am providing. But, does anyone appreciate that? Uh...no.

You're welcome by the way. So, yes I'll take this pack of gum and you wouldn't, by chance, know the way back to the interstate, would you?"

Chapter 17 – Improvisation

Unlike monologues, the next exercise provides little time for thoughts concerning backstory, methodology, or style. This is seat-of-the-pants, reactionary drama that will build abilities for reacting rapidly to those obscure questions often posed in presentations. As with most improvisation groups I have worked with, allow yourself 60 seconds to become familiar with the scenario and briefly develop a strategy.

Also, the content requires interaction with other players. So, find a partner prior to beginning, allowing each other to role play each part.

The ground rules for these improvisations are:

- Time limit is two minutes
- Include all three steps:
  - Setup
  - Elaboration
  - Culmination

Ready? Here we go.

Elevator

It's five o'clock on Friday afternoon at the end of an extremely stressful week. You stand at the elevator waiting for the doors to open when your boss approaches.

Monday, he presented you with data in regards to a proposal due *early* next week. You have not looked at it as you have been up to your ears. After all, he said "next week."

Scenario – Early next week obviously means Monday to the boss, and it meant *review* early next week to you.

Boss – He wants to know the status of your review.

Employee – There is no status to report and needs to buy time.

Backstory – You have promised your spouse a getaway weekend with no work so you know you won't see the data until Monday.

We're moving. Says who?!

Great news! You've been promoted to senior vice-president in charge of a 40-person team. The problem is that the team is in Venezuela and you are in Denver. The challenge is that your mate has been a long-time resident of the current community as has their family. They are a very close family.

Scenario – Something's got to give. Someone has to cave.

Employee – This is the job you've been waiting for. Finally, senior management has noticed you and have entrusted you with this important mission.

Mate – There is no way on earth you plan to relocate across the street much less across the planet.

Backstory – The mate is a very controlling person and will need gentle coaxing and time to think about why they should be on board with this change. Employee has agreed to be relocated in three weeks.

Does this shirt make me look fat?

You're out with your mate, shopping for clothes for a big job interview they have coming up. The need is to look professional yet attractive which is challenging considering shifts in body dimensions recently.

Scenario – While remaining honest, encourage a purchase that is the best possible.

Shopper – You are aware of the *shift* in size but hopeful you can find something to accentuate your figure.

Mate – You are very aware of the topic's sensitivity, but want to make sure to be honest to avoid embarrassment at interview.

Backstory – Your mate can be somewhat of an absolutist—speaking first and thinking later. The shopper is quite sensitive and prone to emotional outbursts.

Who are you talking to?

A casual friend from work has a horrible time with names and an even worse reaction when people remind them of their errors. You are Dave/Donna, depending upon gender, and you have run into them at the mall. You think you know them but are not sure from where. This is a very gregarious individual that feels it necessary to call you by name repeatedly.

Scenario – Without offending, you correct friend of errors in name.

Dave/Donna – You are very aware of the sensitivity issue but quite uncomfortable with the name changes.

Co-worker – You are oblivious to the blunder and very animated about how funny it is to run into each other away from the office.

Backstory – While the co-worker is famous for wrong names, Dave/Donna is really not sure this person knows them at all. It is very awkward.

The reason for the return is?

Your significant other has asked you to return some very personal items to a store specializing in intimate items for the opposite sex. Store policy is that there must be a reason for the return and the items must not have been worn.

Scenario – You are hoping to get this done quietly since you are very uncomfortable and don't like to be the center of attention. Your mate said the items were "binding," thus, the return.

You – Explain the reason given you and hope for the best.

Clerk – Reinforce that the policy is clear; if an item is worn, it is not returnable.

Backstory – Your mate has had issues in the past returning items here and that is why you have been asked to do this instead. You are the mild-mannered one.

Chapter 18 – Now, what?
(Editorially Speaking)

In no way do I presume this to be an exhaustive volume on effective communication and presentations. Instead, it is presented with the anticipated return of enhancing the abilities possessed by all called on to communicate. That would be *everyone,* by the way.

Fundamentally, we are all marketers whether representing a national brand or a brand of our creation, that being who we are. In our efforts to promote greater talking points while providing relevance, I offer these closing thoughts.

Presenting is a fundamental skill delivered by the factory upon arrival on the planet. A baby presents information readily concerning eating, sleeping, and "Hey, clean this up. Are you smelling this?" From those origins, we only enhance the skill set. We present daily in our greetings, our interactions, and, of course, in business settings with designated goals and objectives. Each builds upon the other and allows for evaluation, celebration, or declination depending upon the level of commitment.

On the other hand, at its root, marketing is relationship management. It is developed knowledge that all participants are needed in the fulfillment of stated or assumed goals. Marketing requires the value of everyone involved—not just individual results—but the group dynamic. Effective marketers display similar non-tangibles: integrity, work ethic, and concern for mutual satisfaction as opposed to self-serving narcissism (big word for selfish motivation).

In business, striving to *seal* a deal will result in greater returns than *closing* a deal. As discussed earlier, but worth repeating, seals are hard to break without mutual consent. A closed door, however, only takes a single individual with access to a key and door knob to open. Sealing is much harder and requires effort to ensure that all parties agree on the outcome and will strive to meet the goal. Closing means, "Will that be cash or credit?" While a seal has greater impact on return on investment.

It is important to note that, while my ride in the media world has been one of great excitement, the content here is based on real observations, conversations, and client relations. Years of focus groups, narratives, trial and error, and just talking to people about what really matters were fundamental sources. This material does not represent The Disney Way, nor the teachings and practices of the other major networks I have worked with: NBC, CBS, and ABC.

I hope this material bears fruit for you in your communications and that you are able to glean supportive data along your way personally or in business. For that is the intended goal. Take what works for you and discard what does not. **Mean it like you say it!**

Acknowledgements of Gratitude

No work, great or mediocre, is completed by a single set of hands or the gray matter of one mind. Accepting this as fact, I would find myself remiss for not expressing thanks to many who have helped me along the way and, in no small way, are co-writers of this book.

First, on the business side there are far too many to name, but a collective shout-out needs to be made. You will know who you are as I deliver the attributes. To the ones who taught me that drama was life; that success was a community effort; that programming meant listening; that media was a privilege; that people were the root; that success was not financial but financial must be minded; those that picked me up; those who allowed me to dream even when it turned out to be their nightmare; and to those who said we could: Thanks!

A special shout-out to Melanie, my editor and friend, for making sense of my ramblings and bringing value to my words! You are the wordsmith...I am the rambler. Thanks.

To my friends who have listened to my dreams and called me to action when all I wanted was to rest and think it over; who drank coffee into the wee hours with me and allowed me to fill their world with mine; who insisted that the world needs less dreamers and more doers; and who pushed me off the couch and out the door with confidence to be the latter: Thanks!

Now, on to name calling. To the career military man and his fourth-grade educated wife who told me to name my hill and conquer it; to stand my ground and invite others to share; to find value and worth in all people; to dream impossible dreams but never to believe they were impossible; to strive for all that is right, true, and of value; to never stop trying, for even if you die before you achieve it all, you can never be called a failure...you know them perhaps as Ruth and Bill. I was honored to call them Mom and Dad!

To the brother who left too soon and the sister who holds me in high regard expecting great things…while I question your wisdom, I thank you for pushing me on.

To the in-laws, Hugh and Susan, one with a flair for a story and the other for "get to the point" insistence who brought wisdom on both fronts. From, "It was a cool day" to "Let this day end" style was developed. You are much appreciated.

I also thank the siblings on my wife's side who pushed me to the limit and held me to my word; who listened to my aspirations and had the nerve to believe they could come true. What a group!

To my kids who are second to none—Brian, the oldest, who has become the man we dreamed he'd be, loving husband to Brooke, a gift she truly is, and incredible dad to Campbell and Reid who supply motivation to dream past today. For it is their world that we are molding.

To daughter Elizabeth, the drama queen of our world: Thanks for the reminder that life is exciting and, while it does not always follow the script, it always follows the plan. You are an inspiration beyond words.

Finally, to the one who has stood for decades as the source of all my dreams, who has supported me, corrected me and said, "Yes, you can"; who's heard me snore, complain, and bemoan the unfairness of the ride. She has been my conscience, my motivation, my encourager, my soul mate and, as cliché as it may sound, my best friend. So glad SD said yes to me! Please know, YOU are MY Princess Di!

And, of course, my gratitude to God who placed me here stands alone. May I be found faithful to the call and worthy of the trust.

Press on.....

The Author:

Leon McWhorter, President of McWho Media, llc, (www.mcwhomedia.com) is a published author, playwright, screenwriter and filmmaker with over 30 years experience in marketing/advertising, media/talent training, public and corporate relations. His diverse background with all major networks (NBC, CBS, and ABC), including 16 years with The Walt Disney Company, provided collaboration opportunities with some top creative minds in the industry, allowing him to address varied groups from Los Angeles to Orlando and Chicago to New York. He has served as marketing lead, managing editor, writer, producer, director and cast on stage, screen and on air with seven original stage plays, four original screenplays and literally thousands of radio projects to his credit. Leon has led workshops on the art of communication, marketing, target awareness, writing, directing, acting, public speaking, talent development and improvisation to a wide range of audiences including the National Religious Broadcasters, Texas Association of Broadcasters as well as varied media outlets. He and his wife of many years live happily in Dallas, TX.

NOTE TO THE READER:

For more information go to

http://www.mcwhomedia.com

www.ingramcontent.com/pod-product-compliance
Lightning Source LLC
Chambersburg PA
CBHW020933090426
42736CB00010B/1127